THE SMART COUPLE'S QUOTE BOOK

THE SMART COUPLE QUOTE BOOK

Radically Simple Ways to Avoid Pointless Fights, Have Better Sex, and Build an Indestructible Partnership

JAYSON GADDIS

ISBN: 978-1-63161-032-5

Published by TCK Publishing

www.TCKPublishing.com

Get discounts and special deals on our best selling books at

www.tckpublishing.com/bookdeals

THANK YOU, FRIEND!

By investing in this relationship resource book, you automatically get a couple of bonuses:

A free audio file of me sharing the history of this book, my fears about putting it out there, and why I chose to have this be my first book.

You will also receive an audio reading of ten of my favorite quotes from the book and a deeper explanation of each quote. If you like my actionable insights on the Smart Couple Podcast, this will be a real treat for you.

Just go to **www.relationshipschool.net/smartcouplebonus** to grab your free audio file.

INTRODUCTION

Growing up, I learned about relationships from the school of hard knocks. At no point in my schooling was there a course on how to work out your differences with others. I'm guessing your education came up short in this department, as well. Thus, you learned from your environment, which included adults and peers with a lot of limitations and shortcomings. So you probably learned through painful experience after painful experience and didn't necessarily come to any conclusions that are helping you live a deeply inspired and empowered romantic relationship life. And you may still be going through some of those painful lessons right now.

The purpose of this book is to give you an upgrade in how you see, experience, and live inside of an adult, long-term relationship.

This is not a traditional relationship book that attempts to walk you through a step-by-step process to get a great marriage. Rather, it's a book about the trials, tribulations, and triumphs of partnership.

It's designed to *inspire you* to go deeper—alone and together with your partner. Just by reading a quote or flipping to a random page, you will be challenged, confronted, and inspired to tweak how you see and how you approach your most intimate relationships in life. In doing so, you will move closer and closer to what you want, which, hopefully, is a deeply fulfilling partnership.

My aim is to get you to be more honest with yourself. To take a deeper look inside your mind and your heart. To examine whatever's been "sold" to you about intimacy and love.

This book will challenge you to think differently and, more importantly, act differently. This little book will help you move from being a victim to becoming the author of your life and your relationships.

I'm not going to ask you to change who you are. But I am going to invite you to upgrade and enhance your perception of intimacy and long-term partnership. I'm going to invite you and challenge you to use your relationship as a path for greater self-understanding and self-actualization. I don't want you to be someone you are not. You can't create a great relationship by pretending to be something or someone you think your partner needs. Instead, you'll learn to become a deeper version of who you already are—an authentic, wild, vulnerable, and free human being. Because that's what your partner or future partner ultimately wants, and I'm pretty sure it's what you want, too, if you're honest with yourself.

Once you partner with someone, every day you will have to wake up and deal with two people—the person in the mirror and your partner. Whatever you don't like about yourself will be reflected back to you by your partner. Whatever you don't like about them will become a crack or a bridge, and it will be up to you to choose how you want to play it.

Through the pure magic of partnership, you will see exactly where you are in your development as a human being. I see relationship—and specifically partnership—as the single greatest influence on living a fulfilling life. Like me, you probably don't want to live alone forever, and you certainly don't want to grow old or die alone. If you finally learn how to create a fulfilling and healthy long-term relationship, your life will be greatly enhanced. If you don't, your life will be harder and probably lonelier.

A NOTE ON THE BOOK TITLE

You may have noticed the subtitle of this book (Radically Simple Ways to Avoid Pointless Fights, Have Better Sex, and Build an Indestructible Partnership) captures pain (fighting) and pleasure (sex). Finding the balance between these two is how you create a relationship that is indestructible.

I believe long-term relationships are not a walk in the park. For the brave, partnering with another human being over many years is the ultimate personal growth vehicle, which includes pleasure *and* pain.

While fighting and sex are common parts of a partnership, there are ways to fight well and also to have safer, deeper sex if—and only if—you are willing to embrace discomfort along the way, and get out of your entitled and immature views about what partnership is really about. Eventually you will find that love is earned, not given. Thus, ongoing work is required for any relationship to truly shine.

In Buddhism, there are three aspects to the spiritual path—view, practice, and result. *The Smart Couple Quote Book* is inviting you into a new view (context), asking that you practice (relate, talk, and listen to your partner in new ways), and then the result (an indestructible partnership) will be the fruit of your labor.

It doesn't matter if the result you seek is safety (an emotionally secure relationship), good sex, or just a caring connection, by reading this book, you are one step closer to creating the type of relationship that will last a lifetime.

HOW TO USE THIS BOOK

Rather than write a traditional "how to" guide, I realized that many of us, including me, like to read and consume small "bites" of content to help us think more clearly in a moment of struggle. Blogging, podcasting, Twitter, Facebook, and Instagram allow us to experience someone's reality, and get a hit of laser advice in ten seconds. With so many distractions now, our attention spans have become shorter than ever before.

So, for my first book, I wanted to meet your reptilian brain where it's at, and give you all my best Facebook posts and journal entries about relationships. I have also included some musings from the Smart Couple Podcast, and in the very back of the book, I have included some of my favorite quotes from guests I've had on the podcast. If you are reading the Kindle version of this book, you will find a direct link to each podcast episode if you want deeper insights on that topic.

In a way, this is a teaser book that will give you bite-sized, easily digested morsels of insight and wisdom based on my practical experiences from my own marriage and from working with countless individuals and couples over many years. You can skip around at your own pace and leisure. You might find you need to wrestle with one quote for many days or weeks to understand all that lies within it. I encourage you to read the quotes however you see fit, and I trust you will find something in here that will enlighten you and help you navigate one of the most difficult aspects in your life—partnership. Feel free to share these quotes widely—I just ask that you give them proper credit, and put my name below them.

ACTION STEP

In the Smart Couple podcast, I always include one action step you can do to help you integrate the material and "take it to the streets" in your own life. So here's one action step for you to consider when using this book:

Highlight or put a star beside your favorite quotes, the most confronting ones, or the ones from which you have the most to learn. Then, once a week, on your date night or over coffee/tea, read the quote aloud to your partner, and reflect on how it's going for you, what fears you have, what you want or need, and what you are going to do about it. Wrestle with it, and use it to enhance or deepen your connection. If you get into a fight, relax; that's a good sign because fighting means you are both attempting to work through something together. Repair the upset, and keep coming back to it, and treat it as a *Zen koan* to work with in your partnership. (In the Renzai sect of Zen, a koan is a simple phrase for you to meditate upon and wrestle with until you reach "insight" or an intuitive answer based on your own experience.)

BONUS POINTS

Most couples tend to get isolated when challenges come up. We often don't want other people in our life seeing our relationship pain, so we do what our neighbors do; we put on our happy face and pretend everything's fine. Instead of falling into that trap, challenge yourselves to reach out to one other couple or a group of two to four friends, and begin to share the truths and insights from this book, merely as a way to grow and deepen together. Call it your relationship study pod.

During difficult times, we need each other more than ever. Please don't stay isolated when faced with struggles and challenges. Seek out growth-minded friends and companions for your journey. Remember, your relationship can be a well of resources, giving you added oxygen and nourishment, or it can be the source of added stress and suck the life-force out of you. It's up to you to choose how you want to play.

Enjoy!

SMART COUPLE QUOTES

If you, as a couple, want to unlock your relationship potential and really deepen your love over time, you need to clear the decks, and get to zero. Zero means nothing is under the rug; no more hiding, and all resentments and withholds are aired and cleared. Otherwise, you will spend time getting tripped up by all the baggage that never got resolved. Once you can burn all that baggage to the ground and get to zero, you can actually see each other.

"Oh, there you are!"

"Here I am! Wow!"

But in order to do this, there has to be inspiration, hunger, longing, desire, or... maybe loads of pain.

And in trying to make a big shift, you might find that your early attachment wounds and relationship hurts keep you in a state of ambivalence, fear, or lack of desire. So you stay stuck, complacently sweeping your pain under the rug, or you might think you can't get to a zero. You might think you don't deserve it. You believe lies about your worth and lovability, and you fail to see how beautiful you are, so you settle. You might have no idea what's possible, or you stay in your habitual fog and call it a zero. Patterns and justifications arise, no doubt. I hear you. We all find ways, both conscious and unconscious, to avoid loving ourselves and each other. It seems to be human nature.

And to me, this is the exciting frontier of long-term partnership—where we can see it as a path, a journey, a wild ride back home to who we really are.

Yes, it can be a long, winding road with many twists and turns. Sometimes, it's a circus, and sometimes, a ghost town. The only dead-ends, ironically, are inside me and where I'm blocked. But love appears to be limitless, and some of us, like me, are neophytes on the path. Getting to zero might take us an entire lifetime or a few weeks or years, but what else is there? Why not explore your barriers to love and greater intimacy? Why not explore all of your heart and come to know its vulnerable landscape, no matter how long it takes you? And if we choose to go for zero, let's embrace the waves that take us there. I'm up for the ride. I'm down. I'm in. Are you?

In a long-term relationship, resignation is what happens when we reach an "impasse." When we perceive there's no way forward, we resign ourselves to the situation and say in defeat, "It must not get any better than this," or "I just can't do it." But don't be fooled. There's always a way through; you just haven't found it yet. Can't get there on your own? Hire a skilled therapist or guide to help you through it. And no, you don't need rescuing; you are the perfect person to stand up and keep going because it is your life, your path. Resignation is like an illness. Don't let it take you out. Stand firm. If you persevere, you will find a way through even this spot. You have the heart of a lion, no matter what you've been through. Let that heart push you past resignation into the next chapter. No one is going to save you here but you.

Long-term relationship requires warriorship. If you are not willing to bring that, I don't recommend coming to the game.

Remember: you must train your partner how to love you, how to see you, and how to listen to you. You didn't come with a manual and neither did they; you can't expect them or anyone to just "get it." Getting you takes time and energy. If you and I are in a relationship, getting you requires that I have some basic skills in place that serve to open you. Getting you requires that I know what kinds of things close you, shut you up or shut you down. Getting you requires that I see my own blocks to loving you—that I face what stands in my way, from all of the ways you prefer to be loved by me. Getting you can be complicated, and yet, if I truly care about the dance of love, I will roll up my sleeves, stop complaining, buy some dance shoes, and practice to move with you in a way that inspires us both and lights up a room. That way we can both come to the secure home base of our embrace, and receive deep nourishment that no one else on the planet can provide.

Relationship is like an entire galaxy, where you can explore the truth and nature of reality. In a long-term partnership, you don't need to climb the highest mountain, dive the deepest ocean, or even take a drug. It's all right there, the mysteries of the universe, served up in your face every day by your partner's neurotic and beautiful ways. Somehow, out of seven billion people, you managed—or will manage—to find "the one" who will, after some years, behave and act similar to your parents and siblings. You found the needle in the haystack that will trigger your brightest light and your darkest dark. One day, the adventure is sunny; tomorrow, it's cloudy. You have a blissful week followed by a painful week. And there they are, not even trying to help you grow and evolve...Yet, with the precision of a laser, their behavior will trigger any and all unresolved wounds and scars in you, so you can learn to love just a little bit more. Yes. Your partner is staring back at you, showing you who you are and what you are made of. Helping you see how little you know and how wounded you are. Damn them. But fear not; without even trying, you will consistently return the favor. And so the dance of partnership goes. And if you are weak and have no tools, all of this is a big problem. But if you can find your warrior seat and you're brave enough to play the game in a co-evolving way, your relationship will become the ultimate adventure that teaches you about humanity, love, and Life. Hell, yes, to this vast mystery called LOVE.

When we feel judged or criticized, we stay in defensive postures and feel unsafe to truly open up. So pay close attention to how you are judging your partner. They likely feel it, and it has them contract, just like a child who's getting judged by Mom and Dad. Don't pretend to not judge. We all judge. Instead, use your judgment as a doorway into more self-awareness and more love. More love for you, more love for them. You can't love that place you are judging in them without learning to embrace that same or a similar place in you.

Remember, we can and do grow only when we feel loved. When that judged part of us feels loved, we naturally want to spread our wings and reveal another feather. Our shy, vulnerable desire to be seen can now take another step out of the shadows and into the light.

When you finally draw a line in the sand and choose to be done with your old relationship habits and patterns and choose to learn, grow, get this part of your life dialed, and stop being a victim, it will happen for you. You will grow, transform, and become the person and partner you are capable of being. But it takes courage, willpower, determination, and a fundamental belief that you deserve it. If you can't hold that just yet, I will. I know it without a doubt. Go for it. Make this year the year you grow *through* your baggage to get what you want.

I don't care who you are or what you've been through relationally. It's up to you to face it and deal with it. No one can magically heal your hurt but you. If you really want to have an inspired partnership over time, you'll need to face your pain, over and over. And trust me, you can have what you want, but only if you do the work.

Without friends who see through your small games, you'll keep avoiding a bigger game. Not only that, but your long-term relationship won't ripen over time. Be willing to lose friends. Seek out relationships that challenge you to grow into who you really are, that call you forth into your greatness, that don't tolerate you playing small. I've left friends behind, and friends have left me behind. If you are into evolving and developing yourself, it's just part of the path. If you wanna grow, get used to it. And know that the moment you lose someone, the door will open for you to gain someone new at the level you are wanting to step into.

If you haven't been very good at setting boundaries and you start to put them in place, plan on losing relationships and pissing people off. Don't expect them to get on board and cheer you on. You have trained them for years that you don't set boundaries. All they know is your "yes." They won't be used to your "no." So be patient, and train them about who you are now, today. Start by saying no the next time someone asks something of you. See what happens. Was the experience as bad as you expected? What did you learn about yourself? When you can say no as often as you can say yes, you've made great progress.

A client said to me, "I can kind of ignore my issues when I'm not in a relationship or hanging with someone daily." Yup, I agree. When you isolate yourself and avoid dating or partnership, you don't get triggered with the same precision that a partner brings forth. In the rich container of a long-term partnership like monogamy, however, there is nowhere to run. So if you are single, divorced, widowed, or feeling alone, apply these concepts to family, friends, and co-workers and treat those relationships as "training" yourself for the next partner who will soon show up in your life.

Ever notice the worn-out faces of some of the young parents out there? I get the struggle. Our family was sick a lot when my kids were younger. It can be such a beat-down. Some of you parents look pretty worked over, sleep deprived, and very challenged. And when your partnership with your spouse isn't flowing, the journey can be even harder—it has been for me. I just want you to know, from one parent to another, I see you and appreciate your efforts. I respect you even when you are behaving in ways that are out of your integrity with your own code. In those brutal moments, I respect you even when you are wanting to scream, punch something (yes, even thoughts of hitting your kids), or run away. Even when you are a total disaster, you are still worthy of love and respect. May you go easy on yourself in those moments, while also committing to developing the places in you that need a little work.

If you don't enjoy challenges and learning (specifically, learning about yourself), then you won't like marriage, and marriage won't like you. That's okay; it's not for everyone.

Do the work. If you don't, I can't help you. No one can. The only way to get the exact relationship you want is to bust your fucking ass, and the core of your work is to value yourself like a champion. When you value yourself, nothing can stop you. Partner up and practice. Learn these skills. Stop complaining about him, her, or yourself. Learn to appreciate that amazing person in the mirror. Continue to seek out the very best tools, and then apply them. Don't leave the tool box in the garage and go back to hoping. You're better than that, and if you make excuses such as, "I can't afford it," or "I'm too busy," guess what...? The months and years go by, and guess who will be in the exact same spot? You.

I'll struggle to connect to you if I'm not connected to me.

Hetero-women: Many men remain really confused when it comes to you; he doesn't understand that the very thing he's avoiding (connecting with you), is the thing that could most nourish him. You can help him by not taking it personally when he pulls away, and see if you can stay present and curious. That way, his body will feel into you as a nourishing possibility rather than some kind of anxious, feminine threat. And, if he never gets his act together and works on this with you? Consider moving on.

When it comes to long-term relationship, we're all high maintenance. Even you.

Most of our friends and family members claim they want what's best for us, but below that is the part of them that wants us to play it safe by conforming to their ways and programs. This part of them wants us to not grow, because our growth can polarize and highlight their "stuckness." Our transformation can be quite threatening to them, and they don't even see this is going on. So regardless of their reaction or lack of support, stay true to you… The hidden bonus is that honoring you is the most helpful thing you can do for them and their journey, anyway.

Your partner wants you to be authentic. No one likes being around someone who's disingenuous or hiding. So talk openly about the "shit," and watch your relationship start to get really interesting…so interesting that you actually might pay attention to it.

How much longer will you avoid, run away, and pretend like you've got a certain relationship handled when you don't? It's occupying space/time in your being, and you know this. Go deal. Listen deeper. Get feedback. Go learn about yourself. Start to see that the power is in your hands to change it. The shift starts inside, not outside. Attend to that whisper. Respect it.

Have you noticed that when you don't attend to a relationship challenge, it impacts your health, your sleep, and your focus? That's why it's key to learn tools that clear stuff between you and the other person quickly, so you can keep your precious energy and attention on the things you care about most. So if you have a relational pinch going on somewhere, dig deep, and go deal with it.

Stop wasting time with people who don't support your fullness. Have the clearing conversations to "check it out," and see if your projections are true... "Hey, friend, seems like you don't want me to be so intense. Is that true?" Give them a few examples of times when it felt as if they were uncomfortable with your way. Get what it's like for them when you behave the way you do. Understand their experience. Then, if you confirm that they indeed struggle with your way and you trust your way (including your neurosis), move on, and find people who will cheer on your intensity. Stop apologizing for who you are. Do not spend another day dimming your light because someone's uncomfortable. Some people you know will always be uncomfortable with your way and they will always judge you. Let them go, and keep being you, as you are.

When you love someone, you're willing to challenge them *and* support them. When your partner loves you, you're willing to be challenged by them *and* be supported by them.

Relationship is the fast-track to learning about yourself...and more importantly, loving yourself.

Don't do relationship like you do your finances. In a partnership, if one person is in charge of the finances while the other person numbs out from that part of their life, "because my partner just takes care of it," that couple is limiting their wealth-building potential. Imagine a couple trying to climb a tall mountain; one person would be carrying all their gear and pulling the other partner behind in a sled. Ouch. This setup wouldn't work very long. The same is true in your relationship: both parties need to have an equal stake, and both must pull their weight and work on it.

Your partner is merely a doorway into a deeper reality of how you experience yourself.

As long as you see yourself as broken—you are.

My wife taught me more about relationship than any other teacher or mentor. That is the power of our partner; they help us grow more than anyone in our life. You *must* advocate for what you need, and teach or train your partner how you like to be treated and cared for. Your partner is not superwoman or superman; they can't meet every need. You have to zero-in on what you know they are capable of and what they can realistically do if they stretch themselves. These kinds of interactions require presence and understanding. I need to be realistic in what I ask for without diminishing myself and my needs.

For example: In my experience with people, every human being has the ability to learn how to listen in a way that makes their partner feel understood—so ask for that. Yes, even your partner can do it. It's a basic human need to feel understood by someone we share our life with. This simple skill can be learned by any partner, anywhere, anytime, but they have to want to learn it. You both must place a high enough value on the relationship to get some basic needs met consistently over time. Why settle for anything less and continue to dismiss your needs? It's incredible what's possible when two people consistently learn how to have each other's backs like this over time, and it's available to you.

Apologies are extremely limited. Consider dropping the habitual "I'm sorry," and get more present to what might work better for your partner. Learn how to acknowledge someone in their pain, and own up to how you contributed to it.

If you've truly done the work around your ex, you get to a place where you appreciate them for who they are, and then in your genuine heart of hearts, you can thank them for being who they are and teaching you what they taught you. There is no need to carry your hurt, anger, and bitterness into the next relationship.

Sometimes, our friend or partner is unable and/or unwilling to see their side of a disagreement. This is super frustrating, for sure, but the trustworthy part is that their resistance/avoidance/reluctance puts us back on ourselves to continue to drill down into what opportunity the whole thing is bringing us. This is a very empowering way to play the game. And if our partner continues to refuse to see their side? No problem. We eventually learn that's not the kind of relationship we want to be in, and we move on.

There's only one place to work out our relationship issues—in relationship.

You don't love yourself in isolation. You slowly learn how to embrace more of you by being in a relationship with someone else. They trigger what's disowned in you, so you can own it and love it.

We need to learn how to be accepting of ourselves. We don't need to wait for others to accept us or like us. But we do learn how to accept more of ourselves in our most intimate relationships. Because through my relationship with you I learn to love me.

In a marriage, you wake up every day, asking yourself, "How can I be true to myself *and* serve my partner today? How can I be the best version of myself today? What am I offering him/her today?" If you think love is something that's given to you by another limited person, you're dead-ass wrong. You don't know how to love someone unconditionally, so each day, you wake up and give it your best shot. Stop pretending you know how to love someone. Roll up your sleeves and learn. Listen. Seek to understand them. Look in the mirror, and address your issues as they arise. Deal. Then, slowly, you'll begin to earn a great relationship each day, month, and year because you continue to do the necessary work of learning how to love another human being.

Blame keeps you stuck today, in all ways. Get out from under the blame trap if you want to get somewhere better, brighter, lighter.

"Long-term" relationship means you are in the "long" game. So notice if you keep looking for instant gratification and hoping or grasping for pleasure. That approach leads to loads of suffering in your marriage. Remember... Slow and steady. Highs and lows. Connection and disconnection. Keep being realistic. I think you'll enjoy yourself more.

Not everyone's up for the journey, let alone the *big* journey. But for those few brave ones who are, it's the most extraordinary accomplishment you can experience: to be yourself, to become you, to be you, to live and dance and sing the real you. Life will keep knocking and crushing you until you listen, and your relationships will continue to struggle and limp along, until you face that which you've avoided... Listen, listen, listen. Everything is accurate and aiding you on your path... Turn it all around, and see it as on the way instead of *in* the way.

Thinking about and dwelling upon your relationship issues is a very different game than learning how to deal and to face them head on.

"I want a better relationship!"

I hear you...but wanting it isn't enough. You must set in place concrete action steps to get what you claim you want: take classes, visualize it, read books, study it like a beast, find a mentor who lives it, and get community that holds your feet to the fire. If you don't make "getting a great relationship" a super-high priority by taking these kinds of actions, you simply won't get there.

A big source of human suffering: expecting our partners to be someone they are not, or expecting ourselves to be someone we are not.

Sometimes, we can tell ourselves a story that we don't know what we want relationally... Look again. Underneath your confusion is your longing and total clarity about what you want. Notice the power it holds today. Can you drop into your heart-body for two minutes right now, and feel what you already know? Feel what it longs for and what it wants. Are you willing to listen to it? Are you willing to move through perceived obstacles to honor it? Confusion is fear in disguise. Look deeper. Your inner knowing and clarity is there.

Like the Dalai Lama recently said, "Praying for a better future isn't enough." You need to get off your ass, and do something about it.

The keys to taking a time-out during a fight is letting your partner know: 1. You are coming back, and 2. When you are coming back.

Many people confuse love with infatuation. Love is much bigger than infatuation or hits off the dopamine pipe. Give your relationship a couple of years, and allow yourself to get schooled by your partner—then let's have a conversation about love.

The "work" never stops. If you think you will get through this latest relationship challenge and all will be well, think again. In order to thrive, you have to show up for yourself daily. You must be churning over and growing consistently, or the cobwebs creep in, and you're back to being a victim of your history and somatic nervous-system patterning.

Some coaches naively think that therapy is about focusing on the past, and coaching is focusing on the future. That's fine, but here's the deal—your past is with you in the present all the time; it's in your cells. And until you deal with it, it keeps repeating and showing you where your work is. Weak coaching is about ignoring what's living in your body and pretending you are okay on top of an underground ocean of nervous-system patterning from your childhood that won't get addressed until you address it. Weak therapy is about dwelling on your past and complaining about it. A good middle ground is to find a guide who can help you understand and resolve painful lessons from the past, and use all of it as fuel to become the exceptional human being you already are. Find a hybrid, a blend of challenge and support to get you to the next level.

Your partner's job is to be like a nest. A secure home base from which you can learn to spread your wings and fly.

Be the change. If you want your partner to change, you change. If you want them to open up, you open up. Stop waiting for them to make the first move. The mature person makes the first move in any given moment. That could be you; that could be them. Stop keeping score, and lead.

Part of what has you sustain living inside a very inspired marriage is to take time for yourself to be alone—away from your partner and kids. Do this throughout the week or try spending one night and one day solo every month, at least. It is both healing and helpful. Your solo time is gold. But do the kind of solo time that helps you come back rested and ready to rock it out with your partner or family. Your space to yourself is essential if you want to not resent how "connected" you are. Remember, the definition of intimacy is not "closeness," but rather the balance of closeness and separateness.

Just because your family unconsciously wants you to stay in your role, doesn't mean you have to. Risk being you. They'll be okay.

Men, when you get defensive with your woman you demonstrate and highlight your insecurity. It's far more interesting to discover what you are insecure about; that way it doesn't run your life or ruin your relationship.

What makes intimacy tricky sometimes is that in our attempts to feel seen, heard, and known—which is often what we most desire—we may take a risk, and share who we are in a vulnerable moment with our partner. But instead of being received, we feel misunderstood, judged, and not really heard. Our share triggers them into their "stuff," and now they're not available to us anymore. Sometimes, this can escalate into another fight or put more distance between us. Of course, some version of this is what happened in our families. So here we are again, feeling wrong or bad, frustrated and unmet. Now we might attack, shut down, or second-guess ourselves (or the relationship), none of which are good options for our development. If this is you, you end up feeling defeated, and you might not want to risk sharing your deeper feelings with them again. So what the hell just happened, and how to proceed?

Well, let's play it out as if it were me and you in a relationship...

I got triggered, right? My past prevented me from seeing you. Your vulnerability and the way you shared it reminded me of (fill in the blank—for example: mom, dad, etc.) and I got hooked there. Then you got derailed by me being triggered and went into your stuff, projecting that I was your (fill in the blank—for example: mom, dad, etc.). Now, I'm really triggered because you're reacting just like my mom, and I want to point out how lame you are for derailing this whole thing. You then are so fed up you walk away with your hands in the air, judging me and wondering if you're crazy and why you're with me.

I get triggered by you leaving the conversation because of my abandonment stuff (that I'm not aware of), so I get desperate and try to get you to come back and "work it out" with me. But I'm doing it from a place of panic and charge, so you don't receive it or trust it—as you shouldn't because it's loaded with my baggage. And on and on we go… Can anyone relate to this one?

Yikes! (sound of screeching brakes…)

Both of us need a little love and some help here, yes? I see this dynamic all the time, and it doesn't need to go down this way. At any point, the most mature and resourced person has a responsibility and a choice to own up to what's going on with themselves. Both of us need a shared vision, a shared map, and shared tools. I need "awareness" and the desire to work through the stuff on my side, so I can receive you. You need the same. Both of us have an agreement, which we made ahead of time, that we work on our triggers and hurts that come up in our relationship. I'm committed to my own development and to working through my part. You commit to the same. I'm committed to having you feel understood and received by me. You commit to the same. Why? Because you matter to me. And because I matter to you. Because both of us want to know the other person in an ongoing way.

If having a great relationship matters to us, we will put our time, energy, and resources into relationship development, and never stop working through whatever relationship challenges that arise. We'll remind ourselves that this whole mess isn't personal. We will remember that when we don't choose self-development, we are choosing our childhood habits and patterns, instead.

There's no need to keep carrying anger and hurt with you. But contrary to what the new-agers tell you, you can't just "let it go." The brain and body don't work that way. You can pretend to have let go of something only to find that years later, something triggers you back into that hurt spot, that angry place. Genuine "letting go" is completely doable, but you will need an embodied process and a guide to help you get there. But mark my words, it can be done. You just need the strong desire to reach resolution, and then take bold action to get there.

Being good at relating isn't the same as being good at relationships.

Family relationships can get complicated, and without knowing it, family members can pigeonhole you into your familial role. If you are unaware, you'll slide into it. Years go by, and you wonder why you avoid or resent certain family members. Well, that's your sign that you are wearing your "little kid" pants. So if you are ready to put on your "grown-up" pants, it's time to work on your "differentiation." Differentiation is a psychology term that refers to extracting yourself from your family of origin and becoming you. And no, moving out of state does little to differentiate you from them. You actually need to do the inner work required to tease out who you are from who they are. If you choose to mature in this way, this process will be both painful and liberating.

In the context of a partnership, knowing yourself is not a fixed destination you arrive at one day, where you stop growing because you've reached the summit. It's not a place where you lie to your partner by saying, "I know myself." When it comes to your own self-knowledge, there is no summit. Instead of pretending to know yourself, think of your self-understanding as an unlimited universe. And remember that your partner is here to teach you how to understand yourself even more. This opens up a wider and wider ability to understand others. Let the relationship teach you how to be a student, over and over, and I think you'll find your relationships much more rewarding.

The more you risk exposing your messy and dirty self to your partner, the more you will reap the flowers that grow out of that same dirty messiness.

Men: If you ever feel like your woman is a moving target, she probably is. And if you ever find yourself wanting a predictable, female partner, be careful what you wish for. My wife is far from predictable. She's not simple. She's complex. She's like origami, but just when I figure out her origami pattern, she morphs into a new origami puzzle. Not surprisingly, this frustrates me. Some part of me wants her to be a simple puzzle that I can figure out once, like a Rubik's Cube. That way, I don't have to stay present. I can automate her and check it off my list and tell myself, "I've solved her." The frustrated little boy in me, as well as the grown man, wants it to be easier sometimes. "Can't you be more like me, honey? I'm a solid, predictable guy."

Yet, thankfully, my wife continues to remind me that I am vast, and my love is bigger.

I can continue to learn to embrace her as she is. And what if I never figure out the puzzle and have her mastered? Well, if that's the case, we both win because I stay present and in student mode, which keeps me attentive, listening, searching. Instead of a dull blade, my sword gets sharper over time because I need to stay agile.

The more you develop yourself as a man, the more you can hold your "feminine" partner with love and respect just as she is. So I'm the perfect partner for my wife, as I get to train and practice finding out who she is in this moment and in the next. She shows me exactly where I'm weak. I need this feedback, so I can continue to become who I am. She also helps me teach this relationship stuff with less laziness and more precision because she's not that simple. You are not that simple. Humans are not that simple.

So, brother-man, stay as present as you can with the moving target of your woman, and stop making any of her waves a problem. She's just helping you grow and live into yourself more fully. Instead of complaining, try thanking her.

If you want a great relationship, you'll need to make the relationship a top priority in your life and back up your desire with daily, consistent action.

The foundation of a vibrant, intimate partnership is the experience of feeling connected to each other. This is akin to some kind of attuned flow state between two people. It's a couple's home base. From this fertile connectivity, anything is possible. When two people don't have this kind of connection as a ground to return to, and they don't make it *the* primary issue to focus on, they get distracted and loop in symptomatology.

Attending to the ever-shifting, dynamic, relational current between each other is a daily practice for the committed couple. To work their connection, both parties need to take on, as a devotional practice, their connection to themselves. I'll struggle to connect to you if I'm not connected to me. A couple's core connection requires that both people are committed to their own sovereignty in the relationship (differentiation), while simultaneously attending to the garden between them.

The challenge, of course, is that many couples confuse this core connection with the feelings they experienced during the honeymoon stage, when most things felt good, when both people were emotionally fused in a temporary love fog. They keep trying to come back to that fleeting feeling of fantasy and projection. Both of them get hooked in an immature view of relationship and intimacy. They believe the fairy tales and movies and feel constantly frustrated when they can't return to the warm fuzzies of the first few months. They then get trapped, looking to their partner for their own sense of okay-ness. At some point, they abandon themselves in service of the relationship. When trying to correct this dynamic, they often get very focused on symptoms, rather than the real issue.

Understanding this key distinction moves a lot of couples from frustration to satisfaction if they are up for the real work of relationship.

If your partner has upset you recently and they've made even the slightest bit of effort to repair, acknowledge them for that effort, no matter how small. Thank them for trying, and let them know their efforts matter a lot to you.

For those of us challenged in relationship: Relax. The truth is that most of us have had inadequate training on how to be a mature adult, relationally. Most likely, immature adults trained us, so we can only be what they transmitted to us. So no need to beat ourselves up when we are making a mess or hiding out in our relationships. It's quite normal. That is, until we decide and choose to become mature, and grow ourselves up, thus becoming who we already are. Then with new context, new tools, and new training, we can begin to have more mature, honest relationships. And "mature and honest" isn't what we think it is. Be willing to be surprised. Keep relaxing into that vulnerable, aching heart, and keep learning with great humility.

When it comes to long-term partnership, tone of voice is a big deal. The subtlest of tones can be like lightly plucking a guitar string; your partner feels it, hears it, and registers it in their body. It can shut them down or lift them up, depending on their nervous system's history and memory. So, the next time your partner says you have a tone—even if you think you don't—just try taking their word for it. Remember that your tone is enough to upset them, and it's mimicking a tone that they grew up with; their experience is valid, regardless of what you think your tone is. No need to waste your energy getting defensive, but rather trust they are impacted by your tone of voice. Get their world, validate their feelings, and work on softening your tone even more.

Meanwhile, they can work on not getting hijacked by your tone, and instead, see your tone as an opportunity to heal an old hurt. This way, you are both working on the dynamic together. Because after all, you both want to feel seen and understood.

It is a complete waste of time to get defensive and justify your behavior. Listen, so they feel understood first. Do not move on until they give you the green light, and then once they relax, ask them if they would be up for listening to you and your side.

One of my first relationship mentors said, "Sarcasm stops intimacy." I've never forgotten that and notice how often it's true. When using sarcasm to "connect" with others, notice if it brings you closer or slowly puts up the walls between you. I find that most of the time, it's result is "contracting" rather than expanding. It tends to have a "bite" to it, and it's not serving the deepening process. Humor, on the other hand, tends to bring us closer in a "heart opening" kind of way.

Question from a reader: How do you validate what's going on with your partner without undercutting your reality?

My response: Validating, when done well, doesn't undercut your reality at all. You are validating their reality; that's the point. The way they see things is valid one hundred percent of the time. And remember, their reality isn't *the* reality. It's just them, seeing the world through their subjective filters (like you do). When they feel validated, they relax and soften, which allows them to be in a position to hear you out. So, rather than undercutting your reality, see validation as a window into them understanding your reality even more.

Will you care about yourself enough today to have the hard conversation (you know, the one you've been putting off) with someone? When you continue to withhold something from your partner, you agree to create a rift, a wedge, or a wall between you. Try seeing your uncomfortable truth as a love nugget that will help them grow, even if they get hurt hearing it. You've gotta learn to trust that the deeper part of them wants to know and experience all of you. And believe it or not, somewhere inside, they can handle it.

It is critical to remember, you don't have "the truth" on your partner's experience; only they do. So it's futile to argue about their experience. Instead, learn to understand their experience until they feel understood.

The only way you can have a great relationship is to take responsibility for making it happen. It's in your hands. It's not given to you, but that's the fantasy, that it will be given to you. Yet, once you finally score the one, there are zero guarantees. None. Your partner's commitment to you will wane if you wane in your efforts to stay awake in the relationship.

When in a fight and trying to share your point of view, using, "I always" and "I never" are good signs that you are not even close to telling the truth about your experience. Get in the habit of not using those terms, and instead, go for, "In my experience, you sometimes..." or "From my limited memory, I witness you sometimes..." or "In my experience, X often happens..." or "Through my filters, I remember saying/doing..." Notice how all of these statement leave room for the fact that you don't have an accurate read on what happened. After working with countless couples, I've learned that people rarely get the details right. And the details are not as important as how you are listening to and communicating with your partner. Learn to not get fused to your point of view, and do your best to understand their experience. It will pay huge dividends as you grow together.

My marriage is a Dojo, and sometimes my wife is my master, schooling me where my muscles are weak. Sometimes, I walk out of the Dojo feeling spent, and sometimes I feel alive and engaged in my life, as if I have another foot in, even though moments before I wanted to run away during an arm lock, or when I'm pinned to the metaphorical mat. I'm grateful for her way—she straight-up helps me grow, and growing is what I live for.

Boundaries are essential because when you say no to those self-betraying behaviors and be true to yourself, you get to find out if you will get the genuine connection you're after. My guess is that you want to be with people who can handle you, not people who prefer a smaller, more fearful version of you who is unconsciously taking care of them.

Shame is a brilliant human emotion. It's designed to help us feel like shit, so we do something about it. Our problem is, we add shame on top of the shame pile. But shame in its purest, rawest form is exquisite in its teaching—very precise, very simple, very direct in letting us know where we've veered out of our integrity. Try thanking shame because it's there to get you back in integrity with yourself or to let you know you are subordinating to a fantasy of who you think you should be.

I don't ever recommend doing conflict over text/email. It tends to spark more flames into an already complicated fire. Rather, set a boundary with the other person via text/email: "Hey, I hear you, and I don't work things out with people I care about over text/email. When can you talk by phone or in person?" Then, when they reply with more of their process, kindly remind them about your firm boundary. Don't "bite" and get back into a conversation about the issue. Just say something like, "Hey, as I said, I'm not available to discuss this here in this forum. When can you meet up? I'll respond in person."

I once took two years, trying to process a challenging issue I had with a friend. Two years! Then I finally learned how to get resolution by clearing the issue inside of myself. So if you have "charge" with a non-inner-circle friend and you think you need to process it with them, think again. They may not need anything from you. If you are the one with the charge, it's your responsibility to clear it, with or without them. If it's a very close friend, family member, or lover, then yes, having them there can facilitate a beautiful deepening process by working through the challenge, together, especially if you know what you are doing and if they want resolution, too. But even there, you still don't need them present or available to clear the issue inside yourself. Either way, it's a good idea to learn how to clear the issues on your own because you can never really know what the other person will say or do.

A simple reminder when trying to work out a conflict with your partner is to use, "I heard" rather than "you said." When you pretend you know exactly what your partner said, it typically doesn't go well. I find it preferable to say, "What I remember hearing you say was…" or, "Through my filters, what I heard was…" The benefit to this "responsible communication approach" is the other person—your partner—is less likely to shut down, justify, or get defensive, because you're not telling them you have the truth on what happened. This way, each of you can have your own valid experience of what happened. It opens the door to greater curiosity and listening, which in turn has the likelihood of building safety and connection.

Blame is what you do when you don't know how to
manage or take care of yourself.

If you struggle to say *no* in your family, you'll likely
struggle to say *no* in your other relationships. But that's
okay... your old friend "resentment" will remind you about
how porous your boundaries are, and if you're listening,
you'll get angry enough to do something different.

When you get triggered by your partner today, remember,
it's not about them. Use the power of your mind to
untangle your story about them and what they are doing.
See beyond your smaller, wounded self. See through the
swamp of your wounds. See into what is most true. Your
body has been triggered in the present into having a
reaction to something from your past. Your partner is not
the enemy; that is your confused mind. Learn to re-wire
your thinking, so you can see your partner as a "painful
ally" who wants the same thing you want—to feel loved
and accepted as you are.

Here's my rule of thumb when listening to my wife: I don't
understand her until she feels understood.

Our feelings of inadequacy may show up in our relationships, and we might want to remain small, hide out, or pretend we feel "fine." Understandable. But if you look closely, your relationships are triggering you into your feelings of inadequacy, so you can tackle the very thing that has you feeling this way. Life is asking you to see the wound, face it, and address it. Life is not punishing you. The reason it repeats is so you can master the lesson, move toward wholeness, and then move on to another lesson. As you gear up for the work, commit to seeing your brokenness as your homing device that is asking you to come back to who you actually are. When you start to work with your inadequacy this way, there are no obstacles to you getting stronger.

Irritability is a symptom of a deeper upset happening under the surface. When we don't have permission or tools to get under it, we stay irritable. When you can't find the source of the leak, you'll likely end up pointing the finger outward, like a porcupine moping around defensively. You'll end up making it about external issues, as the real issue festers. You might even need some alcohol or "medication" to take the edge off the low-grade stress you now feel in your body; this only provides temporary relief because you're not addressing what is really going on. Being in a relationship with this type of person is exceptionally challenging, but that's how it is for them on the inside; they are struggling to be in-relationship with themselves. So if this is you, I dare you to face what's below the irritability. You might find a bigger beast. But once you slay this beast, you will be set free, and you might find other people wanting to be close to you instead of being repelled by you.

If you claim you want a better relationship, start by looking for two things in yourself:

1) Themes and 2) Patterns that keep repeating.

Zero in on those two things, and stay curious about each. Learn to identify the patterns that repeat in your relationships (and thus, in you) over and over. This is a sign you're ready for a change. It doesn't mean you will change, but it means the groundwork for your evolution is present. In order to change and evolve past a painful pattern, you'll need to get deadly honest with yourself, admit the pattern is here, remain curious, and have the courage to ask for help. Then you can go do the work required to move through the pattern, using it as a vehicle to get empowered. The choice is yours.

Our old friend denial. Denial is a slippery one; she can cloak herself in a magic dress and paint a rosy picture, or she can turn up the charm to have you think she's there. She loves games like trick or treat, and she eats your ignorance for lunch and feasts off it. Yet, denial is worthy of love, too; denial is often protecting some fragile part of ourselves, and if we expose it too much, too soon, we might crash and burn. Denial merely states, "I am not ready." So next time you judge someone in denial, soften and remember that they are likely not yet ready.

"People pleasers," when you continue to run your childhood habit of pleasing others before yourself, you'll keep manifesting symptoms, such as resentments and other "circumstances" to get you back to you. If you're with a "pleaser," you can help them by not letting them help you. Notice what happens.

Whatever your partner is bringing to you today is something you need; stop resisting it, and see if you can embrace it. Even if it feels rude, mean, hurtful, or overwhelming—consider that you need it for your growth and development. It might turn out you *"need"* to set a boundary with them, leave, or get extra help. You might *need* to be treated poorly, so you can finally stand up and value yourself. Look for the deeper message coming to you in just the right form. It's right on time.

We tend to hyper-focus on the challenge in our intimate partnerships; it can be like tunnel vision. So next time you really get challenged in your relationship, take a few deep breaths—look around in your life, and see who's got your back. Who's supporting you in that moment? See if you can notice that both challenge and support are happening simultaneously. In my relationship life, the more I look, the more I find this to be true. This will soften the charge if you make it a habit.

A lot of people make the mistake that trust is a given in relationships, but even after ten or twenty years, trust still continues to be earned. It can be lost at any moment. It's a fantasy to think that once you get your partner's trust, you can sit on your ass and relax. Stop pretending you're Mr. or Mrs. Trustworthy. We all have parts of us that are not trustworthy, and that's okay. The idea is to develop yourself in your weak areas, so you can earn self-trust, which then allows others to trust you. It's a very entitled position to think our partner should just trust us. No way. Trust is earned continually, day after day, year after year.

"Drama" is for people who have no idea how to do relationship. When you finally learn how to do relationship, the drama ends. Does that mean conflict ends? No. Conflict and drama are two different things. When you don't learn how to navigate conflict well, you incite drama. Drama is for people who resist learning how to face the inevitable tension that arises in any relationship. When you finally choose to learn how to do conflict, you're becoming a mature adult who is willing and able to deal with interpersonal challenges, and any drama fades into the background.

"He always gets defensive anytime I bring up anything." This is the kind of statement we say when we are triggered. Notice the black-and-white thinking here, and see if you can get under this, and be more honest about him. For example: "Sometimes, he gets defensive when I bring up difficult subjects." This statement then turns the attention on you. When he "gets defensive," what gets triggered in you? Check in with how you are speaking to him, and try relaxing a bit more. Examine why you've attracted a "defensive" partner.

The degree to which we value ourselves is the degree to which other people value us.

It's my bias that, in a long-term partnership, both parties need a small handful of support outside the marriage. The insecure, isolated couple has nowhere to turn during the fight except to their partner. And as some of you have found out through your own experience, that's complicated. It isn't always effective or efficient. The person triggered by you will struggle to support you in the heat of the moment. Yes, they can learn over time, but expecting them to show up for you if they are triggered by you will prove difficult, initially. Going at it alone during a fight is also limited. Thus, we need community.

We each need a pit crew to hold us during our struggle. The kind of team that is able to hold both of us in love and respect. This kind of quality support does not mean a person who goes along with our story about how lame our partner is. That's not support. The support I'm talking about is people who can validate our feelings/experience and who *also* challenge us to see our own side of the issue. For example, it's likely we are not seeing something about ourselves. We are stuck in self-blame or blaming others. We may be looping in an old pattern and can't get to the roots of our trigger, which can, and often does, change the game. Quality friends and guides with shared context and tools can help us see what we are not seeing. So, find at least one trusted ally outside your relationship who will both support you *and* challenge you in your time of need.

Sometimes, your friends want you to stay small; they want you to not be so serious, so intense. Sometimes, they might even try to get you to relax and chill with them. "Why do you have to be so serious?" they might ask. Sometimes, they might tell you to lighten up, and have more fun. But if you're on a mission and you love to grow, there is no other way to be than the way you are, just as you are. If you are living out your inspired mission, then you are having the time of your life, and everything you do, including working all day, is nothing but fun! In fact, it's the most exhilarating ride to be on. At a certain point, your gaze becomes so fixed on your goal that nothing will stand in your way. The critical friend or foe comments or silent judgments will only become the glue that solidifies the deep trust you have in yourself. So, be you, and stand strong in that, and always use other people's judgments as fuel to go to the next level.

"I want to learn how to avoid triggering his anger when I just need him to hear me and be present and rational." First, I wouldn't spend a lot of time trying to control something outside of you, like your partner's emotions. That's next to impossible. Instead, see his anger as an opportunity for you to get more okay with your anger and with anger in general. This opens the door to being okay with conflict, which helps you learn to stand your ground, and stand up for what you care about and need. Finally, you describe your need, but it's about him. "I need him to hear me." Instead, try to reframe your need, and make it an actual need of yours, such as being understood. "I just need to feel understood by him." See the difference? See how his anger is opening a door here, not shutting one.

Relationship is like a musical instrument; the more I learn about it, the vaster the instrument becomes. Will I ever master relationship? Maybe not...but I'm on the path, and the more I dance and practice with it, the more music I get to play.

When you get emotional in your marriage or partnership, relax. Just feel the emotions like a wave, and let them wash through you. They won't kill you. Seriously. And definitely don't make big relationship decisions when you are emotional. Relax again. Wait until you have a level head, a stable mind. Then make a choice.

I rejected women for years, but when I took a closer look, I was rejecting the uncomfortable feelings and traits these women provoked in me that I didn't like. I was rejecting certain "feminine" qualities I had, such as my sensitivity, my emotional life, my empathy, and my vast heart connection. So I was rejecting an essential part of myself. Check in with yourself; what is your partner triggering in you that, if you look closely, you're probably rejecting inside yourself? A fulfilling, long-term relationship will require that you own what is disowned. Your partner will always trigger you. Relax, and learn to play the ownership game, and you'll find your relationship improves.

Try not to make your partner's reactions be the reason you can't be yourself today. Risk being you, regardless of how they receive it. If not now, when?

Feeling understood takes two people. If you don't feel understood, part of that might be your partner's listening skills, and part of it is probably your communication skills. It is critical to learn how to explain and to speak about your experience in a way others can digest, hear, and reflect back. Equally important is your partner's ability to listen in order to "get you," as well as their commitment to getting you. This is simply a skill a couple can learn over time, and once both parties learn it, frustrations around feeling misunderstood become rare, little bumps instead of deal-breakers that could cost you the relationship.

I appreciate you single parents out there—seriously, big respect. Specifically, the single parents who don't get to "tag out" when the other co-parent or partner takes over. I've been with my kids for four days without their mom; it heightened the notion that I am my kid's personal assistant 24/7. I laughed out loud a few times this weekend at the designed brilliance in parenting to strip away any notion of "me." They are two little gurus, and I am their devotee, and overall, it's a breeze because I'm madly in love. But I'm human, and at times, I just want to take a shit alone or sip my tea for two minutes in peace. They have shown me where I'm limited, again. It's very helpful, and I know I'm stronger through this experience. I think that scab on my face has been shaved down a bit, thanks to those little beings.

The moment you disconnect from your relationship pain, you disconnect from yourself and your journey. You've lost the battle because you're turning your back on yourself and essentially saying, "I can't do my life. I can't do this moment. I cannot be me." You've allowed your self-doubt to win. So if this is you, consider the possibility that you are much stronger than this. You can indeed meet your life. You are the very person who can do it because it's happening to you. There is a warrior inside you who is totally up for this crazy, painful life. Dig deep inside, and don't allow fear or self-doubt to win. It's your life. Your hero's journey. Still can't do it? Get help. Reach out to one person right now, ideally your partner if you have one, own that you are struggling, and ask them to believe in you. Look them straight in the eye, and say, "Hey, I'm stuck in my self-doubt and fear, and I need you to believe in me. Will you just say to me out loud, 'I believe in you', and please only say it if you truly mean it?" If they can't say this to you, get someone who can and will say it and mean it. Hire someone, pay someone. And your work is to take their words, those words that are outside of you, and ingest them, swallow them. Eat those words for lunch and digest them. Just like a small child who is afraid and doesn't know, sometimes, you need the outside to tell you it's okay and that you can do it. But in the end, you *must* tell this to yourself and believe it. You must do whatever it takes to find that little voice inside, that inner knowing, and blow on it like an ember until the flame gets brighter.

Your work is to meet your pain, learn from it, and then burn it to the ground with your massive heart. Whatever current relationship pain you are facing will keep knocking on your door until you do. That is your work. Stop running. Go do it.

If you are experiencing relationship pain in this moment, pause and take a breath. See if you can relax into a different perspective; consider that whatever pain you are experiencing is trying to help you. Your pain is trying to help you to come back home to who you are and what you are here to do, and to embrace more of you. When you were young, you created strategies to get love. Pain helps you break old strategies, get out of fantasies, and be on this earth—right here, right now—living more authentically in relationship. Pain helps you come back to a less-fabricated, less-complicated, more honest you. Welcome to the profound path of relationship.

You're never fighting about "stupid stuff." The silly, surface symptoms always lead back to a main artery. If you are smart and paying attention and willing, you can get to the "gusher" that will change your relationship dynamic. But you'll need to be willing to go there—right to the jugular— instead of getting caught by the surface arguments. Look deeper, roll up your heart-sleeves, and deal.

If you want a better relationship and you actually do the work, you will fall apart. You will come unglued. You will feel pain. You can't avoid what is true. So, relax. There's no problem with pain. None. Pain helps you grow. I call it relational growing pains. The sooner you get on board with this and embrace the growing pains, the sooner you'll get what you want. Ask yourself if you want the pain you are currently experiencing by avoiding whatever you're avoiding. Or do you want the pain that comes with a big reward because you were willing to face it and work through it? Choose.

Whenever my son is "acting out," there is one remedy that gets him back in line—get connected. In other words, if he's behaving in a way that challenges me, my wife, or his sister, I can almost be sure that our connection has waned and is not as strong as it could be. So the best solution is to get outside, just him and me, and find our flow, find our connection.

For example, this weekend, we went on an adventure out in nature. One of our favorite activities is to look for animals—animal signs, birds, feathers, cool rocks, bugs, trees, and anything that is amazing to us. It was bumpy, at first, but then we slowly found each other. We first saw an owl, then caught frogs, and eventually, we found this feather, or it found us. We've still got a ways to go, but we're getting there; his behavior is a wonderful reflection of our attachment, as he continually teaches me where I'm not present or attuned. Humbling and helpful. I love him so.

All of us have the capacity to learn how to do relationship well. It's not just for people who are smart, successful, or good-looking. A great relationship is something even you can get, no matter who you are or what you've been through. You just have to want it and be willing to put in the effort.

Dwelling on your story and "poor-me-ing" yourself isn't growth, nor is it directly experiencing pain. Dwelling is fearfully staying comfortably stuck in your head and keeping you right where you are. Be honest; a part of you doesn't want to do the work and wants an easy fix here, or perhaps you want someone to rescue you from your situation. I hear you. This is why we medicate our pain away rather than embrace it and grow from it. So, instead of dwelling, try feeling. That's right. Feel your direct experience of upset or pain in your body. Go in there and feel every corner of it. Learn how. Learn to be with the emotional landscape, so you can learn from it. Ironically, the more directly you can deal with your experience, the sooner the strong sensations and emotions abate. Yes, this takes courage and warriorship, and you can do it.

Marriage in isolation—while socially hiding our struggles—is a recipe for more pain over the long haul. Community support is critical to the health and vitality of a marriage. For example, when I'm stuck, the men in my life love the shit out of her (and me) by helping me see where I'm blocked. A light bulb goes on, behavior shifts, and now I can return to her more available, ready, and able to own my side. I'm now more resourced and can tend to the fire of my marriage in a whole new way.

Advanced relationship work is about seeing that we are at war with ourselves. This is the real issue. Yes, it appears that we are at war with the outside, but the real shift comes from the inside; the healing is in here. If I bridge the gap in here, I bridge the gap out there. This is raw, nitty-gritty, and real. It's not about the other person, but we need to go there to mine the gold in here. I blame you, so I can discover and uncover what I've disowned, which you represent. Once I do this, I walk through a gateway into more freedom and empowerment, and relationships become less and less complicated.

When we burn some relational issue to the ground, the ashes become part of the rich soil and fertilizer that helps us integrate that old part and helps us to grow stronger. Our roots can extend a bit farther into the soil, our limbs can reach a bit more sunlight and water. This awakens a bit more confidence in ourselves to be all that we are. So keep burning, keep burning.

Next time you are triggered by your partner, say thank you. Why? Because they are helping you grow.

None of us need "too much." We need exactly what we need. However, as kids, we may have learned to be fiercely independent and stuff our needs so as to not upset the big people. This makes it tricky and challenging to have needs and then express them with our partner in an adult relationship. But I can assure you there are some hidden needs in all of us, even you. See if you can find at least one need this week, and express it. Not once but every day, or as often as you are feeling it. Treat it like exercise, some kind of daily workout. Practice owning your need(s) in a consistent way. As you get more honest and own your genuine need (that will likely never go away), you slowly begin to train your partner in a new way. Up to this point, you have trained them that you don't have this need, so they have agreed to not attend to this part of you, which is why they might react or resist at first. Don't blame them for not reading your mind and meeting that need when you haven't been willing to tell them in a consistent, steady way. Your relational need deserves to be met, and it's up to you and your partner to co-explore this terrain, and educate each other about your valid needs. If you judge yourself or them as "too needy," you'll keep this painful cycle operating underground, and your needs (that will never go away) will remain unmet. So get in there, take a risk, have the hard conversation, stay vulnerable, and go practice owning that valid need.

It's so satisfying to come out the other side of a big rift or fight with my partner. It seems to me that we continually "earn" our way back into connection. It's not given to you just because you found the one. In fact, if you think you don't have to continually "earn it" with your partner, it will be just a matter of time before you don't have a partner anymore.

The more you can sit with your discomfort, the stronger you are in a relationship—because challenges never go away. Learn to be with upset and challenge, and you'll win over time.

I too used to complain about emotional women, until I realized I had disowned the one living inside me.

Don't settle. If we're talking about marriage, you are choosing your lover, your teacher, and your best friend on the planet, all rolled into one. This is a very big decision. Take your time because this same person will show you exactly where you are weak, helpless, and afraid. They will also show you how magnificent you are and ask that you keep stepping into that. By making this grand choice, realize you are saying yes to all their history and the baggage they carry, most of which you won't even see initially because they are blind to it as well. You will be the person who brings it all out into the open. And they will bring out your unprocessed emotion, hidden traumas, and the scared animal you'd rather they not see.

The bottom line is that both of you will be shown how little you know about love, intimacy, and relationship. What you thought you knew about love will be burned to the ground, and a tiny pile of ashes will be left in the ashtray of your fantasies. You'll be invited to face all of you, which will finally humble you to learn about love. If you don't want this amazing, alchemical blender, then don't bother coming to the long-term-relationship table. If you are up for the raw, unpolished, messy love found in monogamy, choose wisely, my friends, as your best and worst will be revealed, and it will be nothing short of a true hero's journey.

When we hide out and don't tell the truth in our relationships, we set ourselves up for all kinds of drama that then gets us to come back to truth, to the core, to our integrity. So you can't lose. Life will guide you back to your center through the pain and pleasure of your relationships. Your body will yell, whisper, and scream at you. Your job is to listen like an astute disciple of this majesty called Life. Listen like a curious, willing child...and the next step will appear.

Do *not* settle for less than a strong connection. Don't go after a fantasy, either. You can't be in happy-land all the time. A strong connection is one where you feel as if you are a heart-centered and heart-connected team in the midst of financial stress, parenting stress, sexual struggles, fighting, distancing, and the rest of life's challenges. All of your "stressors" are opportunities for the two of you to strengthen your bond as a team. Don't allow things to pull you apart, and don't blame yourselves or each other. Stay in the fire; tend to it daily. Do not give up on your heart's longing to be known and feel held more deeply. It can happen if—and this is a *big* if—you *both* work at it daily. Put serious attention on making your home base strong, and nothing will stop you.

Every single time I am challenged in my relationship, I have a choice: complain and blame, or dig deep and grow through it. Fortunately for me (and sometimes after a short tantrum), I always choose the latter, and I end up stronger as a result.

A lot of folks, including me, get trapped into thinking that intimacy equals closeness. But if any of us are paying attention to ourselves, we see the setup in that. If we see intimacy through this perspective, we spend vast amounts of energy denying, rejecting, or judging ourselves around our need for space and separateness. Some of us might even become co-dependent or emotionally fused with our partner in our denial of this fundamental need. Instead of this kind of one-sided intimacy, let's embrace the other side—separateness. Then ask ourselves, "How do I accept these seemingly contradictory energies at the same time rather than pretend to be all about closeness?" It is critical, if we want long-term, vibrant intimacy, that we heed the words of Bruce Tift, and come to know and accept intimacy as a balancing act between separateness and closeness.

You've got to see conflict not as a problem, but as an opportunity to deepen and enhance your connection.

Like it or not, the state of adult sexuality in this culture is that of a wounded, teenage boy or girl. We have a lot of work to do here if we want to be in a mutually empowered and inspired sexual relationship with our partner. So please get honest with yourself and your partner, and if this resonates—that you have some work to do—then go do it. Don't let shame or your fear run you here. Push yourself to grow in this area. Your partner will thank you.

I remember speaking with yet another person who was proud of the fact that she has never fought in a relationship. Major red flag, folks. Get your head out of the sand, and stop compartmentalizing your baggage. Thinking you have a conflict-free relationship suggests one of two things: Either you are still in the honeymoon phase (enjoy it while it lasts), or you are ignorant of your own disturbance and are asleep in your relationship, comfortably coasting along on autopilot, clueless to the grand design and massive opportunity to be found within your partnership... There is no such thing as a conflict-free relationship. There *is* such a thing as a person who is consciously or unconsciously avoiding conflict. And that person is you if you claim to never fight. To fight is to live and to be human. Conflict will help shape and sculpt you into more of who you are if you embrace it.

Most people are unconsciously trying to regulate their nervous system from the outside. This is appropriate and normal. In fact, this is critical in infant development; as babies, we "attune" to our external environment. If the big people and our environment are safe, we feel safe inside. If it isn't safe, we don't feel safe inside. As we grow, we attract into our lives the ongoing vibration of our own nervous system. So if we are anxious, we attract more of that. If we are hypervigilant, we attract things that mirror or require hypervigilance. If we are "negative," we attract that. If we are calm and relaxed, that is mirrored back to us. The trick from an adult attachment perspective is to learn to co-regulate each other, consciously and out in the open. Once you begin to learn how to regulate your partner openly, a new world opens up.

If I see something as only my partner's fault, I remain a helpless victim of my circumstances rather than a mature adult who can and will get into the driver's seat of his or her empowerment.

Most fights are due to a values clash: you are expecting them to live like you, and they are expecting you to live like them. If you claim you know your partner and you fight a lot, try eating some humble pie and consider that you don't know them very well. Re-commit to understanding them and what they care about. Then learn how to communicate in terms of what they care about, not what you care about.

JAYSON GADDIS

If you want more ease in your intimate relationship, say no
to drama and yes to conflict.

The relationship results you are getting are directly
proportional to your ability to do conflict and be with your
reactivity during upset. For example, I get in the ring. I
throw some punches. I get knocked out. I want to bail,
but...I get back up. I learn. I engage again. I fall down. I get
my ass kicked, and I get back up *again*. I can feel that
familiar pattern of wanting to exit, but I stay, instead. I stay
in the ring, and I learn again. This time, I see a new horizon,
a new angle, something I have not seen before. Ah, ha, yes!
I look down and notice my feet planted firmly on the
ground. I get a few stiff uppercuts to the chin, but I'm still
standing—not budging this time. A new stance, a new
belief in myself...rooted. This time, I remember to put in
regular, consistent practice and hard work. It's beginning
to pay off. Right, I showed up daily. I didn't run or collapse
or posture into some false, intellectual belief in myself, and
thus, I'm arriving anew. And the bonus of this level of
practice is that just below the surface, your brain is
rewiring itself through your hard work to give you a new,
more rewarding relationship experience.

There are two main options when it comes to dealing with your emotions in your relationship. One, we can use them to run our "poor-me" story, and keep the faucet on, staying in our victim seat, which is a *huge* waste of energy. Or, If we truly want to get empowered, we can use the rawness of our emotions to bring us back to our heart and to greater alignment. In other words, our emotions are feedback, helping us come back home to our integrity. I think you'll prefer the latter.

Our issues are only a broken record when we are asleep to them. Once we wake up and see what's really going on, our "issues" become a song of opportunity.

Conflict is just another doorway to love.

When you feel disconnected from yourself or your partner, have you noticed that your addictive behaviors increase? This is a painfully good discovery that will help us get to know ourselves. The first and best remedy against addictive behaviors is to get reconnected, back to you, your body, your heart. You might find that meditation or yoga helps you reconnect. Or maybe journaling, walking, or nature time helps. But I find the best way to connect to myself is to connect to you—to look into your eyes—and to my vulnerability. I might want to tell you as I look into your eyes about my fear, shame, or stuckness. This will help me come back to us. When this approach clicks, you will feel connected again because you are willing to find out what vulnerable, uncomfortable feeling you were avoiding. Just own it, feel it, and be seen in it.

Your relationship is supposed to suck until you face your baggage that the relationship is triggering...Once you begin to face it, your relationship will take on more color, more meaning, and be more fulfilling

Please remember...if you leave one relationship due to whatever your negative perceptions are about the other person or yourself and you don't address those challenges, you will repeat the pattern down the road with a new person in a new way until you "work through" the issue on your side. So, dig deep inside and always ask, "What is my part in this dynamic?"

We are all intense to be with in a long-term relationship. Just give it time. Once you sober up from the "Kool-Aid" of the honeymoon period and you stay in the game, it's on. Your inner jerk or fearful victim will come out, and sooner or later, your ugliness will probably upset your partner...a lot. And if you don't have any tools for the bumpy road ahead, you're in for a lot of pain. No one escapes showing the other person their darkness, their unconscious, their victim, their party pooper, their jarhead, their asshole. It's just part of the program. And it's not really a problem if you learn how to deal.

From a reader in regards to conflict: "I want to know when to let things slide... When do you let it go, and when do you lean into conflict?" My response: I never let things slide. I'm a sensitive creature, and it works better for me to honor any ripple, and work through it. When you don't approach conflict this way, any unresolved issue—no matter how small—gets stored in the brain and body and then adds to your allostatic load. You're more likely to blow up easily, and over time, you are run by your jacked-up nervous system. So...my bias is to deal with it one hundred percent of the time.

Symptoms of avoiding conflict: affairs, pain, shallowness and stagnancy in other relationships, judging, criticizing, trying to change your partner, training others to get used to your mask, dead marriages, stale connections, lukewarm love, compartmentalization ("tuck it away in that box over there, then I won't have to..."), friends and buddies who stunt your personal and spiritual development. Yikes. That's a lot, right? So, decide if you are going to fall prey to one or all of the above, or if you are going to strap on your big boy or big girl pants, and learn how to do conflict.

Fighting in your marriage is essential. Get used to it. Once you embrace fighting, you relax, knowing that conflict is unavoidable. Now you're available to learn. And when you finally learn, you get more resilient, agile, and pleasant to be around.

When we're disconnected from ourselves, we tend to hurt those we love. We say mean things, we do stupid shit, we threaten, we run away, we blame. All these are signs of you disconnecting from yourself. So the work is to come back to you. Come back into your body, back into your heart and out of your fearful habitual thinking. You see, your partner is just like you; they struggle, too, they get disconnected, too, and they are doing their job by triggering you into your stuff, so you can face your baggage and heal it. First, you have to get some tools and a great framework to change your behavior, and learn how to connect, and come back home to you. When we are connected to ourselves, loving isn't a mystery.

Couples who perpetually struggle see challenges as problems and want them to go away. Couples who flourish have one thing in common—they face what is true, learn to see challenges as opportunities, and they choose to grow from all of it.

When I decided to get married, I decided to grow up. When I had kids, I decided to grow up some more. Starting my family has been the most challenging and rewarding part of my life to date. And growing up has never felt so damn good.

Within every conflict is the seed of more understanding and closeness.

See if you can stop comparing your relationship to other people's relationships. Most couples are wearing a mask, only putting their best face on around you. If you followed them home and put a spy cam on them for a few days, you'd see they are no different from you—struggling to connect, living in a haze of tension, having surface-level connections, tackling logistics, brushing things under the rug, pounding sugar, avoiding, blaming, having scheduled sex, avoiding sex, having some great moments and having some shitty ones. The truly courageous couple is willing to talk openly about their problems and challenges because it's what's going on. Plus, by admitting weaknesses, you have no choice but to work on them. When you avoid admitting what's going on, you trap yourself in a no-win model because you show no respect for the struggle. You are demonstrating you are caught in a fantasy that you shouldn't be struggling and that everything should just feel good. You won't allow yourself the dignity of asking for help. Smart couples, on the other hand, admit that partnership is quite hard. They are willing to discuss the struggle and even seek out support and guidance when they get stuck. This couple gets that unless they are willing to learn and grow, they probably don't stand a chance at making it. This couple chooses to face and overcome challenges, so they can find their way into a thriving, mutually loving partnership. So remember, everyone is just like you—struggling in their relationship. But you can be different by telling the truth...inside and outside. Once you do this, you buy a ticket out of the fearful status quo, and you begin the journey of earning a fulfilling partnership over time that includes and honors the struggle.

When we do anything other than our soul's purpose, we are bound to suffer until we get aligned.

If your partner goes silent on you, just keep giving them space. Send the message with your whole being: "I'm here and available when you are ready." Eventually, your partner will come around. Space does wonders. Pressure doesn't.

Sometimes, I feel shut down and resistant. If I'm not careful, I might get seduced into making it about something "out there." I entertain that for a short while, and then it's time to come back. For me, "the return" is mostly about making contact with something I'm resisting or moving away from inside of me...about finding my way into my heart, into my vulnerability, and back into relationship. Once I drop below any story and make contact with that thing I was distancing myself from, I'm back again. I'm more honest, more pleasant to be around, more willing, and more available to my life.

There's really only one framework—seriously, only one— that will give you long-term, mutually empowered, marriage success. That is for both of you to embrace a personal growth and development mindset. Couples who don't grow in an ongoing way don't make it.

One of the most common ways to increase the likelihood of you feeling like shit is to compare yourself to other people. Comparing is supposed to feel terrible. Not because you are a loser, dumb, or inadequate in some fundamental way, but rather you feel like "ass," so you can come back to being you, to your life, and to your brilliance. Don't entertain those untrue stories. There is no need to feed those feelings that keep you stuck. It's a waste of energy. Shake that off, stop pretending to be where someone else is, and be you, right where you are, beginning, learning, and growing.

Guess what happens if you don't learn to take space in your intimate relationship? You unconsciously begin to seek space by creating a fight, distancing yourself, or making "excuses" to get your necessary space quotient. This indirect approach is trustworthy and fine but typically creates more drama in your relationship. If you want to avoid creating more pain *while* taking space, be direct, proactive, and don't confuse intimacy for closeness. Intimacy equals closeness *and* separateness.

When I sense my partner is withdrawing and our connection is compromised, instead of saying, "What's wrong?" I prefer to make an observation about our connection. "Hey, I'm not feeling as connected to you, and I'm curious what's happening between us?" Try it out, and see what you notice.

Whatever relationship pain I'm currently experiencing is happening for a very accurate reason. It's designed to wake me up out of my habitual patterns and get me back into alignment with who I really am. Even though it's uncomfortable and often burns, it's trustworthy, right on time, and I'm grateful for it.

Relational cut-offs are painful. When anyone you care about "goes away" and stops talking to you, it can sting. And there's some gold in their silence if you look closely in the mirror.

If you think you have to work something out with a friend or co-worker and you keep trying to get them to understand something or meet you halfway and they keep ignoring you, blowing you off, or not responding in a way you prefer—then drop it. When people don't want to "work it out" with us, consider it good news. This is feedback that it's time to work it out in yourself. Any issue with anyone can be dealt with alone. You really don't need the other party to get to resolution. Of course, if it's an intimate partner, it's a different deal.

When you get married, you are deciding to go into business with someone. If you don't see your marriage like a business, your business will limp along and likely go under.

The distinction between caring for someone and care-taking them is essential to learn. When you care-take someone, you are being careful. It's often fueled by an unconscious fear of them being upset with you if you don't help them in the way you assume they need help; this is typically what you did as a child to get love. Whereas, caring for someone implies you are willing to challenge and support them—even ask them before offering if they need something from you. When you care about someone, you respect their choices and don't need them to be different in order for you to feel okay. It's subtle, but start noticing the difference.

Avoiding your issues is what gives them power.

Notice your "barriers" to entry. What barriers do you unconsciously put up that keep you from the kind of relationships you want? It's really not "out there" as much as you want to believe. That's the disempowered seat. You're bigger, brighter, and smarter. Take a look under the hood of yourself, then you're already a step closer to what you claim you want.

The only way to continue to build a bridge with your partner is to face yourself. It's a choice. And when you don't choose to face you, you'll eventually turn away from them.

It was the deep disconnection in my life that ultimately led me to find deep connection.

When I want you to live according to my values and priorities, I create an expectation of you, and when you don't meet it—which, invariably, you won't—I get pissed. My anger is just the feedback I need to stop laying my trips on you, and instead, learn to love you as you are. Thanks, anger, I knew you had my back.

When I'm in a fight with my partner, it's my responsibility to get out of it and then milk it for every morsel of growth that's in it for me.

After you share and your partner says, "I totally understand you," pause and listen to yourself. Ask yourself, "Do I feel understood?" If not, push back, and let them know. "Well, I don't feel totally understood." Then ask for clarification: "How do you understand what it is that I'm experiencing?" If they come back and try again, that's a good sign. If they get defensive and don't want to review that for you, you just triggered an insecurity of theirs. Oh, boy. They have a button around not getting it right. That's okay. Ask them to slow down, and before you go into what just came up for them, see if they are willing to stay with you right now, and finish that thread. If it's important to you, you will keep advocating for yourself around feeling understood. "Hey, honey, wait, I'd like to finish with me first before we move on to you, okay?" Why bother with all the little details? Because you are sensitive, and your feelings and experience matter. Because it hurts to not feel understood or gotten by the person we are closest to. My guess is that you want to be with someone who looks after you, sees you, and understands you. So advocate in order to feel understood, and don't stop until you get it. You deserve that.

When you lose your connection to yourself, plan on losing your connection with your partner.

Sometimes in a marriage, you just want space, a lot of space—like "leaving the relationship" kind of space. If you're normal, you'll feel trapped sometimes, and you'll probably have the "grass is greener somewhere else" thought whisk through your mind. However, staying in the fire will help you differentiate between your fear (of closeness, which often comes from your past) and a genuine need (for space, which will help you do intimacy even better). Space is essential in a long-term partnership, so learn how to take it in a way that honors and deepens the relationship.

Running away from your partner or relationship problems is understandable. I hear you. I sometimes need a break, too. However, we both know the issue won't go anywhere. So do your very best to face what you've been running from, and develop the "chops" to return in a shorter amount of time than you typically do. I'm pretty sure this will help you get closer to what you want.

Your fear, combined with liking someone a lot, creates an interesting combination. Fear can breed even more insecurity, which, ironically, doesn't help the security of the relationship. So it's in your best interest to work with the places you feel fear and insecurity, so you can have what you really want—a secure relationship.

The dopamine of the first few months is amazing! Enjoy it while it lasts. You see, part of infatuation's function is to keep you in the dark about your partner's shadowy faults, so you can procreate and keep your DNA alive. But be patient, grasshopper... Soon, you will do something to provoke their dark side, and you will get a whiff of their true colors. Now, as you sober up, a fuller, more realistic picture of them will emerge. You want this, so you know what you're dealing with and can choose wisely about the partner you want to join forces with. And if you choose to walk away in mild disgust after seeing more of who they actually are, know that your projections will subside until the next partner emerges with their baggage hidden behind their gorgeous veneer. No matter how hard you try or how smart you are, you can't outsmart the fact that you'll attract your disowned parts, again and again, until you embrace the truth of how relationships work.

Men, if you want less drama in your relationship, you must learn how to validate your woman's feelings and experience. You've gotta learn to listen to her with more of your senses and faculties. And when you do, you'll see she's not that complicated. You're just a stubborn ass sometimes, like me. Own that, then set down your ego and listen like a beast until she says, "Thank you. I feel understood." Do this, and you're on your way to much less drama and a much sexier woman.

Shutting down isn't a problem. It's a smart, adaptive survival response when you feel threatened in some way. Often, it's how quickly you "come back" or "return" after your shut down that can be problematic. Thus, it's considerate toward your partner if you work on quickening your response time after the shutdown. For example, I used to stay shut down for weeks. I remember one time, I was shut down for at least two months in a relationship (some people go years!). Then once I started working on my shit, I decreased that time to a week. Then a day. Then hours. Then minutes. Sometimes, depending on the issue, I can still shut down for a day or two, but my commitment is always to return to myself and my primary relationship. Returning and getting connected again is so essential because life just sucks when I feel this way, and I'm a drag to be around. I'm invested in returning to my partner in a way that has us both feeling connected to each other. If you have a family, it's wise to come back to them as soon as possible also. When I'm shut down, no matter how magical my kids are, their "way" can feel annoying, and I'm the edgy, grumpy dad. In these moments, I feel like Homer Simpson, fumbling around fatherhood. This makes for really bad parenting. So, no need to judge your shutdown. It's normal. However, do make a commitment to shrinking your response time with your partner or family. I'm pretty sure your partner will appreciate the effort, and your family vibe will become strong again.

In a long-term relationship, you must find your way while being you; otherwise, you'll keep trading who you are for connection, all the while resenting your partner.

Our relationship patterns are extremely trustworthy; they are our old friends and allies. Just like a spotlight that won't turn off. Seriously. If we pay close attention, we'll keep getting the information we need to transmute them. They won't go away until we learn to work through the pattern.

When I expect you to be like me (which is a habit of mine), you'll disappoint me nearly every time. That helps me come back to my journey, and re-invest that energy inside my own space, inside my own heart. Ah, here I am again! Since there are many critters, dragons, and beasts on this road, I'll need that fuel for the battles that lie ahead. So, thank you, for not being like me.

If you're the one with a need, it's up to you to ask for it. Don't expect your partner to be a mind-reader.

Marriage is like eating an apple. At first, it's ripe, juicy, and delicious. But after a few bites, you eventually hit the worm. Around the worm is the bruise or the wound that tastes bitter, sour, or rotten. If you don't like worms, which is understandable, you'll toss this apple, and go get a new one. But in marriage, there will always be a worm or two. There will always be a rotten part you want to avoid. But if you are smart, you'll realize that every relationship has a worm, and that worm serves a vital function. You will come to learn that the worm is not a problem at all. In fact, the worm, when treated properly, can help grow a new apple tree. Any farmer knows how vital good worms are. Attend to the worms, and watch your marriage grow strong.

In long-term relationships, saying, "I'm sorry" is extremely limited. Sorry is a necessary and important step in human development. It is what little kids say after they hurt a friend or sibling, and it's essential to learn. But just leaning on I'm sorry in an adult relationship rarely helps another person relax and feel safe again with you. It just won't cut it for the nervous system to relax. Instead, you'll need to step up your game, and take ownership of what you've done. It is also paramount to get and acknowledge the impact your behavior has on your partner. Doing these two things instead of resorting to your habitual apologies will go a lot further toward strengthening your relationship and repairing your severed connection. Your partner will notice the difference and thank you.

There's a big difference between blaming yourself and taking responsibility for your part. Blaming yourself is you running your self-hatred trips on yourself, and in the end, that goes nowhere. Taking responsibility for what you did or didn't do helps you get in the driver's seat of your relationship dynamic; it puts you in charge of changing it, which is why most people would rather blame themselves or someone else for their relationship problems. Again, this gets you nowhere—so learn. Please, learn. Learn the strong skill of taking personal responsibility for what you want in your relationship. When you do this, you will get what you want over time. It's up to no one else but you.

When I disconnect from my wife, I am reminded of how precious our connection is. However, our connection doesn't come back automatically; that would be a very entitled relational stance. Instead, I earn my way back into a clean and clear connection by facing my triggers and challenges.

You can't hide from your partner, but you are welcome to try. However, you should know that by hiding who you are, you rob your partner of the chance to know you more deeply and to make choices accordingly. Couples who hide erode the safety and security of the relationship over time. Plus, if you're both honest, you both know you're hiding on some level because you are afraid to bring the truth. You're afraid to bring more of you. You have self-judgments and shame that are running you now. Understandable yet limited. So if you claim you want to be loved, then learn how to reveal yourself by taking a risk. Start small, and work your way up to more authentic expression. It's hard to love what's not being revealed.

We all feel inadequate at times in our primary relationship. But typically this shows up as anger or checking out because we don't want to relate to the feelings of inadequacy. Low grade anger can even turn into depression and can cover over this sense of inadequacy because we repress and suppress the more uncomfortable feeling or belief down below. But if we allow ourselves to "go there" and we stay very honest, we feel inadequate because we have not yet reached the level of competency or mastery we desire. This is what the student feels sometimes, on their way to learning something. Seen in this way, our inadequacy reminds us where we actually are on a journey toward something, and this opens a door. If we can stop expecting ourselves to be farther along, we can relax into where we are...right here, right now. Instead of my emotions being a problem, they can serve as a painful reminder to stop comparing, stop expecting, and stay in the fire of learning and growing right where we are.

When you're triggered by your partner, don't distract yourself. Sit in the fire of your experience, and see where it takes you.

Marriage, as it's practiced in this culture, is dead. Unless, of course, you come in with the view that it is a path and not some bullshit fantasy. Then marriage is an endless landscape for growth, evolution, and learning about what love really is. Redefine it for yourselves, and don't let people who have bad experiences with marriage tell you how it's going to be for you.

Some therapists or psychology "experts" have been known to say that shame is a useless emotion. Not true. There is no emotion that is useless. Shame is your ally. Shame is feedback to help you get back in your integrity with you. Shame helps you come back home. Shame helps you see when you are subordinating and comparing yourself to unrealistic fantasies and expectations. Shame, my friends, is your friend. And no, you'll never be able to get rid of it, because as with all emotions, it has an innate, useful intelligence to it. Welcome shame, and learn from it.

We all have an enemy—someone we compete with, judge quietly, or hate. This takes up vital and precious internal resources of ours. Notice how much energy you are giving to that person and how much they are in your life, even though you'd rather they disappear forever. Take a good, hard look, and be honest, and see that the trigger is inside you. Once you discover this, ask yourself if you want to keep walling off that part of you (because that's what you are doing). Finally, what are you going to do to get complete with them without their help? Remember, you don't need them to close the loop. It can be closed inside you. Your choice. Carry that sore spot around, or face it in yourself and be free?

A dynamic with my son as a father...
I feel the tension of the working parent. Being an entrepreneur and a part-time stay-at-home dad, I get to choose my schedule. It's amazing...I've been very fortunate. I'm so grateful for my wife and the way we do it. And recently, I am choosing to work more and parent less, and my son is impacted. He's used to having me around more, and he's also going through other normal developmental transitions. The behavior change in him is very subtle, but I see it every day. He's acting out more, he's more aggressive, more distant with me, and he's easily hurt by me.

He's five, so he doesn't have a lot of adult words for what's going on for him. Regardless, I've been focused on him and his behavior and trying to help him use words more than shouting, tantrums, or hitting. He tells me I'm "always" mad at him. Interesting. I read that as his way of saying, "Dad, I'm mad at you for not playing with me as much and working more. Under my anger, I'm hurt, my feelings are hurt. Help!" Mostly, I've been focused on the challenging behavior in him, instead of my own process with our changing dynamic.

Just today, it hit me even more. I dropped into some deep sadness over choosing to play with him less... It felt like a punch in the gut, but I got it. I then shed some big tears and felt the tension of wanting to be in both places at the same time. I want to be home all the time for every second of my children's lives, *and* I want to be working all the time because I love my job. I'm guessing this is a universal experience for many parents who are deeply connected to their kids. I'm vulnerable, and resting humbly in what feels like unresolvable tension that is mine to embrace.

Sometimes, people judge you directly and give you unsolicited feedback. If you are in an insecure spot, it may "go in" and hurt, but if you are resourced, you can let it roll off your beautiful skin—because it's not really about you. Your "way" is triggering them into something important that they are unlikely to face, and that's okay. When you get some distance, you can sift through their sloppy delivery to see if they have a valid point or a grain of truth directed your way. There is no need to collapse or even apologize. You are learning, too. You're a work in progress, like everyone else. Simply find that soft spot in your heart, and thank them to their face or quietly in your ever-evolving mind and heart.

No matter where you are in your life or what you are doing, people are judging you, so you might as well do exactly what you want to do.

As long as I put the responsibility on someone else, I'm helpless to do anything about it, and I don't have to change anything about myself.

You attract your opposite to integrate and to find balance.

Throwing small tantrums can feel self-righteously good in the moment, but have you ever noticed that once you get that out of your system, it can lead to yet another strong emotion—feelings of shame. Doah! You just added some more pain to the pile! But in this case shame is very helpful. Your shame reminds you that you're out of integrity with yourself or someone else's expectations of you. That's right. Both anger and shame are actually just feedback loops to get you to come back to your center. Anger highlights where you're expecting you or someone to live according to your values and priorities. As you get familiar with anger and shame, you'll start to experience new insights. Light bulbs will come on and more choices will open up. So, feel free to throw that tantrum and know that you have an internal trustworthy feedback loop designed to help you behave in ways that are more aligned with who you actually are.

Do you feel as though you have to get permission from your partner to do something, be something, or say something? If so, that's a good sign you're headed toward a resentment. Perhaps it's time to give yourself permission to do exactly what you want to do, while considering your partner's feelings. The question you want to ask yourself is, "How can I do what I want to do, while having my partner's back?" If both parties embrace this attitude, you can expand, dance, and grow together in an expansive way.

If you are angry or frustrated with your partner, relax out of focusing on them, and go directly inside your body. Take off the label or story of "frustration," and feel the sensation as energy moving through your body. Ride it like a wave, so you're not afraid of strong somatic sensation. Next, quietly get curious, and explore what their behavior triggers in you. Look at your expectations squarely in the eye. Ask yourself, "What are my expectations of him/her? Are they realistic?" Get clear and decide if you want to keep putting those expectations on them. Get their input. Find out if they are okay with your expectations and if they are up for meeting them. If not, change your expectations, notice your anger dissipate, and watch your connection improve.

I read some really bad relationship advice the other day. The person basically said something along the lines of, "If you resent your partner, just end it." Yikes! I completely disagree. Resenting someone is not their issue, it's yours. And while you'll get some temporary relief by leaving them, your resentment will still be with you—like a long tail dragging behind you—until you deal with it. So start seeing resentments as amazing opportunities to face yourself, grow, and get closer to your partner.

If you sit on the sidelines and complain about the relationship pain you're in and then look to someone else to alleviate that pain, you won't get anywhere. Best to face the person in the mirror.

I hear this one a lot: "I've spent a lot of my marriage trying to be the person he wants me to be." What does this lead to? Big resentments due to big self-betrayal. When we try to be who they want us to be, it only serves to keep us small, safe, and stuck in our fearful self. It seems to me the work of a long-term relationship is to continually learn how to be who we are. I mean, who we *really* are. And when we willingly take steps over and over to be our genuine selves, the reward becomes greater levels of personal alignment, satisfaction, and empowerment.

When you resent someone, look closely. You've likely done
one of three things:
1. Projected unrealistic expectations onto them
2. Forgotten to set a boundary
3. Failed to advocate for yourself

It's easy to want a relationship without strife or struggle,
and it's a whole different story to go against your inner
hedonist in order to learn and to earn a deeply fulfilling
relationship—one that embraces both the pain and the
pleasure. It's not a fantasy. It's earthy, dirty, and dark. It
smells and tastes like fresh soil, loaded with shit, nutrients,
and worms, and it's as rewarding as that luscious, green
garden you worked so hard to create and will regularly
feast on. But you have to attend to it daily to keep out the
critters, bugs, and weeds that want to dine on your efforts
(or lack thereof), and after a period of growth (if you've
been attentive), there's a harvest. Enjoy it because then
your garden will die and become compost. The newest
season's issues churn over to create the fertile soil for next
year's crop. Sometimes, these "seasons" can happen within
days or weeks, and this rapid life-cycle of the relationship
is not a problem for the ever-evolving couple. Life and
death. Challenge and support. Fun and not so fun. Happy
and sad. Connected and disconnected. So get some tools,
stay present to it all, and...enjoy!

If you keep using "I'm sorry" to repair after challenges in your relationship, you'll notice how, over time, it works less and less. We humans need more than this. Consider dropping the habitual response, and get more present to what might work better for your partner. If you want more bang for your buck, learn how to acknowledge someone in their pain, and own up to how you contributed to it.

When you get triggered and upset by your partner's actions or inactions, what is the old, stand-by default behavior that you resort to? Be honest. Examples include: shut down, go silent, freeze, attack, get defensive, check out, food, sugar, alcohol, Facebook... When you get upset, it is important to know what you consistently choose. Do you fight more? Check out? Run away? Shut down? By knowing what your pattern is, you can slowly educate your partner about it. This helps them to avoid making you wrong for your pattern. It could help them be more patient with you. It could lead to more understanding between the two of you. It might even help you work through the pattern. In a partnership, it is essential to know what happens when both of you get triggered and to be able to co-support each other getting stronger there. You can keep reacting the way you did in your childhood, or you can help each other slowly grow up over time.

When you get married, you are going into business with someone. You are agreeing to set up shop in your spouse's lap—their family, their space, their darkness, and the most awfully annoying parts of them. They are signing up to see your hatred, your judgmentalism, your cynic, your demon, and your ugliness, too. It's one of the best places to see a person's true colors. It's the ultimate personal growth tool, which helps you learn to love and embrace all of these parts in you and in them. Read that again—it's *the* place to learn how to love another human being, which in turn helps you love and embrace yourself. So ask yourself, "Am I really willing to experience this?" If not, I don't recommend long-term partnership. And even if you are up for it, you'll need to learn how. How does one work with the monsters inside and outside? Start by working with your reactivity and upset in a way that empowers you versus collapsing into your patterns of defense and misery. Who's in?

Try this in your primary relationship, and see where it takes you. "My daily practice is to love you as you are."

Our childhood strategies are like a glass ceiling on our relationship potential. Work through the issue from your past, and watch your ceiling evaporate and your relationship expand.

It's always fascinating to me when I'm stuck in a challenging moment with my wife, how I can look at her and feel my closed heart and hurt, and then in the same exact moment, turn two feet to my right and face my son or daughter and feel open, soft, and loving. Two feet apart, and I have a completely different experience occurring in the same heart, in the same moment. What's going on here? Is my wife just mean or cold? Does my heart or love have a bias?

It's more like my heart has a stored memory of unhealed pain that my wife's "way" triggers. Because I have a lengthy history with her—and with my parents before her—it makes sense that I can contract during a fight with her. My kids haven't hurt me in the same way, so my heart is more resilient and open as I turn toward them. And I could continue this observation by "pointing" my heart toward anyone whose behavior hurt me and notice the same sensitivity going on. Open here, closed over there. Unsafe here, safe over there.

This is the intelligence and precision of the human heart...showing me where I'm still partial, where I have yet to embrace, where I'm still hurt, and where there's pain that needs love. Our fights invite me to embrace another piece of shrapnel from my past, rusty and neglected from an old hurt, ready to be noticed, healed, and integrated. After sitting in tears this morning with my family at my side, I relax in gratitude for my smart, vulnerable, and tender human heart.

When we are triggered and stay upset, we become less and less attractive. We collapse, shut down, get mean, hide out, and defend. Have you noticed how you actually morph into a semi-ugly version of yourself? By not coming back as soon as we are able, we drive our partner away. It's human nature to turn away from the ugly beast, and it's in our best interest to "get on it," and come back to ourselves. Come back to that wise, bold heart, to the inspiring person we are, so we can return to our partner. And if you are the non-ugly partner, you might as well try to love their ugly, triggered beast—that, too, is good for your relationship.

It's in the deepest, longest night of the winter that I celebrate you, darkness, for it is only when I am aware of you that I can feel and so appreciate your contrasting friend, the light. May we all see the light in the mirror, and stop rejecting the dark or making it wrong inside us. Let's embrace both. Thank you, nature, for reflecting back who I am and who we are—love.

Sometimes, there is no fanfare in relationship. No fireworks. No magic. Just the low hum of a steady current between you and your partner. Rather than make any of this wrong, see if you can listen below the hum. What is there? What is in your heart? What is really going on? Listen some more, and see if you can feel the edge of vulnerability in all of it. Then simply share what you notice with your partner—see what happens next.

At a certain point in a long-term relationship, you realize it's not the other person. Your attempts at blaming, positioning, dodging, and weaving come to a whispering and gentle poof. That is a beautiful day, and from here on out, you will experience a different kind of freedom.

You'd be surprised about how many relationship "experts" and therapists are not empowered in their own marriage or relationship. Do your homework. Who's a living example of what you want? Go seek out that person.

When you're in a relationship, and find yourself trying to be who your partner wants you to be, you'll end up failing at that game, no matter how good you are at pleasing other people or how hard you try. This makes us depressed over time, and we will inevitably feel bad about ourselves because we can never be an expert at being someone else. Hopefully, we'll fail every time; this kind of pain is helpful because it gets us back to who we are. So relax into being you, as you are, not despite your partner but for them.

The guide is inside.

Truth—sometimes, I doubt myself. Sometimes, I feel off center and out of sorts, but then...I feel into how I parent. I feel oxygen rush into my lungs, and my heart lifts. I see these bright, little lights that are my kids, and I grow taller. My pride swells, and I feel like a lion—a lion that is ferocious and powerful, and, at the same time, soft and supple. This balance feels amazing in my being. My kids awaken the dormant playfulness in me, the vibrant, spontaneous innocence, the unending love that I would die for, and the powerhouse protector. My doubt fades, and I relax, knowing I am a lion.

The degree to which I trust others is the degree to which I trust myself.

You don't need to work that hard to have someone choose you. If you are working hard to get someone to love you, you are wasting valuable energy and resources internally. Feel free to keep repeating this pattern, as it may burn out in time. At some point, however, you'll grow tired, resentful, and fed up, and you'll do something different. If you want to speed up the process, reel your attention away from your project of trying to get them to be different, and bring it back to the project of loving and embracing your beauty and awesomeness right now. Stand tall, and find your dignity. You don't need to settle for scraps or change your partner. Trust me, you can have what you want, and all you need to do is accept *you* as you are.

Sometimes, people want something from me. They want time with me, lunch, a call, help, or whatever it may be. You have people wanting the same stuff from you, right? And I can guarantee you that sometimes, you "give yourself away" when you don't really want to. I can relate. Often, I'm a yes, and other times I'm a no. When I trust my "no" and then have the courage to follow through with it by setting a boundary with them, they can react. Their reaction can be small or big, mean-spirited or full of blame, (which affirms why I had a gut feeling about setting a boundary in the first place.) And if I'm honest, I have that place in me that wants to cave, just so I don't have to deal with their reaction and have them dislike me. But if I listen to that young part of me, I will betray myself and then resent them for "taking" my time from me. Grrr. Instead, even though it's risky, I'd rather trust myself, and learn to be okay with feeling uncomfortable and being disliked. What about you?

Growing beyond our patterns is essential if we want to live an inspired life. For those of us who feel challenged a lot, it's important to understand why we keep attracting stressful, traumatic, repeating events or certain people into our lives. Most people think that it's our bad luck, bad karma, or perhaps it's someone else's fault that our path feels so hard. We might look for a target to blame for our misery. We might slowly slip into the victim seat and even collapse.

However, if we investigate deeply about this, we start to realize we are attracting that vibration into our lives for a reason—to repair and update the old hard drive—and it's up to us to get out of our pain. In other words, if we catch on, we use the "unsafe" environment as a wake-up call to seek higher ground. We realize our patterns hurt us, and the developmental task in that moment is to get in the driver's seat and renovate and retrain the rusty wires from the inside out. During this process, we can find people and environments that are safe and that can hold us with love and respect through this growth period and over the long haul. We can seek out people who are running a different, higher vibration than we are, and we can attune to that. But those types of people don't typically come into our lives until we take responsibility for our outdated default setting. If we do rise to the occasion, we can now find the right people because we are doing something about it. Eventually, as we pass through this portal in our soul's evolution, we no longer need to keep attracting old, painful experiences in the same way. We have crossed over this particular threshold. The sun comes out, and our vision is wider. We can hold more. We can see more. Having passed through this, we stand stronger in ourselves and are more whole. A nervous system upgrade. Confidence through hard-won experience. At last, we are demonstrating that we are ready for the next stage in our development. And then? Another painful pattern will surface to call us deeper into who we are. This is called mature human development.

Disconnection in marriage is normal, even necessary.
However, it's how you fight, repair, and return that makes
all the difference.

When your co-workers get one version of you (the
pleasant one), and you come home and your partner gets
another version of you (the unpleasant one), this is a sure
sign you are either living an internal lie or living outside
your current abilities and skill-set. This invites pain to
come your way, so you can learn to be *one* person, not two.
If this is happening in your life, first be honest. Tell a close
friend and then your partner. Be honest that you might be
living a lie. Do this, and you're on your way to becoming
the same person, the person you're here to be.

Someone once reminded me what bullshit it is when
people say, "Once you find the *right person*, a relationship
won't be hard work." This is indeed total and utter bullshit.
The "right" person for you is the person you are with—the
one who is triggering you in exactly the right places you
need in order to get stronger as a human being. Period.
That doesn't mean you have to stay with that person, but it
does mean they have a vast ocean of growth to offer you (if
you choose to play your relationship this way). So...want
more suffering? Stay stuck in the childish fantasy that it's
supposed to feel good all the time.

I leave friendships not because I think I'm better than those people but because I value myself. As I grow, my self-worth grows. Turns out, I also have a core need to be met, seen, and known in my very close relationships. My friendships that can't (for whatever reason) meet this need, become less nourishing, and I slowly lose interest. I spend less and less time with those people, and eventually, I leave those relationships behind. My rate of growth exceeds their ability to hang with me. If I didn't value myself here, I'd probably "hang in there," feeling unknown and underappreciated by those friends and wondering why I'm avoiding their emails or calls. Notice this in your own life and what you are doing about it. The growing person must leave people behind; it's a fact. There is no way around it. If you don't get on board with this, your "friends" will hold you back, and over time, you'll resent those relationships and wonder why. If you don't like loss, then don't grow.

Psst... Stop. Take a look in the mirror...The person staring back at you has some baggage. Your partner will help you bring it out. It's okay; we all have it. So, relax. You're not that special, just like the rest of us. But do yourself—and them—a favor, and please don't turn away from your pain or what they trigger in you. If you do that, you lose. If you face and learn to embrace the man or woman in the mirror, you're on your way to a great relationship!

If you keep thinking relationship is going to bring you happiness, think again. Sure, it will bring that sometimes, and it will also bring the other side: sadness, hurt, pain, and anger. If you embrace all of it, you'll not only be on your way to a fulfilling relationship, you'll enjoy the ride more.

Sometimes, when we have judgements toward someone, we might want to give them some feedback, but we hold back. We might want them to do something different, but we don't say anything. We judge their choices or behavior and keep quiet. We stuff it so as not to upset them. We put on a friendly face and bury our true feelings. We know we could really rock the boat and lose this relationship if we spoke our truth. Then one day, we break up. The relationship or friendship drifts or ends entirely. And now that we have some distance and the relationship is more or less over, we come out with our hidden truth. We finally tell them how we really feel. I call this "lobbing a grenade on the way out," and it's a cowardly move. We do this because now we have nothing to lose. The relationship, the thing we feared losing the most, is over, so we feel justified in letting them have it. And because we carried a hidden resentment and want to offload it, rather than face the fact that we were too scared to speak up, we find a way to blame them for our silence. But this behavior speaks to how scared we are to speak our truth when the stakes are higher in a more committed relationship. Rather than point the finger at some normal human being who might have reacted to our truth, let's take more responsibility for our fears and risk speaking up when we have everything to lose, and trust the relationship can handle it. And if it doesn't? Well, wouldn't you want that information?

When you expect your family to get you, to make the choices you make, or to be considerate like you are—you set yourself up for loads and loads of frustration and strife. They can't and won't conform to your ways. However, there is one thing you can count on them for: to live their life according to what matters most to them.

Most of us move a little too fast when triggered, and that's when we tend to make it worse. Training yourself over time to slow it down can work wonders. Even if you're a person who gets quiet and shuts down, this can still help you. Practice when triggered. Challenge yourself to pause for a count of five then take one huge breath, and relax your shoulders. Don't speak yet...relax some more...now respond.

Where is the absolute worst place to get relationship advice? Friends and family members. Unless, of course, they live and breathe what you aspire to, and you know for certain they live it daily. Going to family for relationship advice is like asking them if they can help you navigate an Everest climb. No way. They have no idea what they are talking about. When it comes to relationship, they haven't studied human beings for decades formally, and they are not trained to help people with their inner-most relationship problems—they are of little use here. They may be able to help you with art, real estate, your golf game, picking out a great restaurant, or teaching you about acupuncture, and all the things they are an expert in. But unless they study themselves and human beings for a living, they are pretty useless in the relationship department. Seek people who live and breathe relationship problems and how to overcome them.

I'm so grateful for my wife and kids. They keep me in check in so many areas, and without them I wonder if I would work 24/7, spin out, and kill myself in the process. I love the balance family brings. I love how I get slowed down. I love the demand for presence, for honesty, and for my embodied heart. Thank you, family. Thank you for keeping me here, on Earth, in this life, in this moment. Grateful. So grateful.

Contrary to popular belief, fighting with an intimate partner a lot is a good sign, but only if you are into growth and development. Intense fighting means you have tremendous opportunities to grow and develop yourself with this exact person. They trigger you in ways that are very upsetting, which points you with laser-like clarity to the issues you need to go work on in yourself. So, if you want to end the war "out there," you'll need to end the war "inside." Then you'll earn your way to an outstanding relationship.

It's pretty damn amazing what a parent will do for their child. Sometimes, when my kids ask me for another piece of toast, I suddenly stop and trip out on the fact that I'm a server in the restaurant of my home. I've been making toast—or some other form of breakfast—for them for seven years, every single day. That's about 2,555 mornings! Then if you add in the other two meals a day my wife and I make for them, that's 7,665 meals, not counting snacks. Holy shit! Day in and day out.

"Sure, I'll be completely responsible for you. Brush your teeth, wash your body, clean your clothes, feed you, put you to sleep, and respond to most of your requests throughout the day for the last 2,500 days. No problem, honey." Why? Not only because I'm completely responsible for my children, but I am completely devoted to them and their well-being. They're not old enough to care for themselves, and they're even helpless sometimes. But I've got their back. I'm here for them.

There is no day off when parenting little ones. There is no exit. No escape. None. But, thank God, I have a solid partner to tag in when I need to tag out. And it's incredible that I don't resent my kids, although I do want to kick their asses sometimes. The bottom line here is that I just sit back in awe that I am a total servant to them and their (nearly) every need. I'm incredulous when I stop and reflect on it. Then there's the magic of how they unintentionally "serve" it up to me in my development as a human being, just by being exactly as they are. Wow. Humble pie. Bowing to the built-in intelligence and this deep act of relentless service called parenting.

Comparison is unavoidable. However, it's in our best interest to avoid it as much as we can, and stay in our lane, focused on our life, our mission, our work, step by step, day by day. When we compare, we get emotional. It often shows up as anger toward them or ourselves. When we look closer, we're mad because we expect to have it all together and to be farther along than we actually are. This is our entitled self, thinking that Life should just give us accolades, expertise, knowledge, and status. This frustration is understandable. Watch kids do art. Sometimes, a child will expect to produce a masterpiece of art and make it look real, but it is next to impossible when they haven't trained for years as an artist. Like a kid, we can sometimes throw an internal or external tantrum when things don't turn out the way we want them to right away. We have forgotten there is a journey to make, effort to put forward, and hard work involved. Comparison only serves to deflate you, unless, of course, you can learn how to use something you admire in them as a way to get inspired yourself.

If I could only transmit one thing to my kids, I would model to them how to do intimate relationships. Why? Because our closest relationships determine the quality of a well-lived life.

It's your fear of being alone that keeps you stuck with someone who doesn't treat you with love and respect consistently over time. The irony here is that you already feel alone inside your relationship, so you are afraid of what you are already experiencing. Which fear do you prefer? And which one will get you to a great relationship sooner?

We all need community. The power of being seen as we are, warts and all, is so potent—yet so few have it. There seems to be a pervasive preference to be happy or upbeat around our so-called communities; we wouldn't want to upset folks too much and make people uncomfortable, right? Yet, I think we both know that doesn't feel authentic or good. Know you are not alone in your relationship pain and struggle. No one is above that. Find community. See if you are willing to take a risk with your people, and share what's really going on. Doing so might even take your friendships deeper.

Whoever you are judging or pushing away right now has got valuable information for you. They are indirectly asking you to reclaim that part—the part you judge. Keep running, or look in the mirror and deal. Your choice.

When you are quietly holding back in a group context (work, family, in a classroom, etc.) ask yourself why. Then ask yourself if you want to be known or seen in your experience and if you feel you have something of value to contribute to the leader or other group members. If the answer is yes, it's now your responsibility to engage. There's only one guaranteed thing that can happen— learning. You can't lose.

Your relationship has to be a high enough priority that you can drop what you are doing, and show up for your partner. What's more important than your secure home base? You consistently do this for each other, over and over. It never ends. Unless you have a fantasy that your challenges will stop. If you resent them because you keep showing up for them and they don't return the favor, then you've got a different problem, and I'd recommend dealing with it. If showing up for them feels like a "should," then you're trapped in "obligation," and resentment will help you get out of that lame game. The trick is to learn the fine dance of being there for them without losing who you are or what you care about. Can you be there for you *and* them in a way that works for everyone, in a way that builds trust, strengthens your bond, and fosters mutual love and respect? Yes. I'm certain you can.

It's not about staying together. We see people stay in lame jobs they hate every day, and that is true in marriage, as well. Sticking it out just because your culture tells you it's better is nonsense. Get out of morality and other people telling you what's better or worse for you. Feel into what's right for you, and claim it.

Anyone who is divorced and still stuck in blame is demonstrating they are still in their wound.

I don't recommend getting married unless you are ready to face all of you. Anyone who has been married for more than five years gets this. Sure, you can try to hide, but hopefully, your partner will sniff you out and bring forward your darkness, your wounds, and your brightest light. There is so much power in the long-term road of relationship. Don't do it unless you want to be seen in all your glory.

Next time you find yourself judging some guy who has shut down, take a closer look. He's probably in severe pain and has no idea how to get out.

A question from a reader: Should an empowered man require understanding of his needs/masculine perspective from his partner, or is it his job as an evolving man to learn to be the source of understanding for himself, his wife, and his family?

My answer: Of course. While *require* is a strong word, if my wife couldn't understand me, I wouldn't be with her. That's a basic requirement in my marriage—"striving for mutual understanding." A desire to "get" each other and a fierce commitment to do so.

I shut down my emotions for years, and many are like me. If you are a "shutter downer," educate yourself on the steep cost—that is, if you are even aware you're doing it.

Fear is so interesting. It can grab you by the balls (er...or something else...) and yet, somewhere inside yourself you can find a place to face it—all of it. Fear, discomfort, and vulnerability are part of the path of the warrior. So set your sights on a bigger vision for yourself, and get ready to be uncomfortable. No need to freak out...just feel it, stay present, and take another step forward.

After fourteen years of being with my wife and having two kids, when I'm not paying attention, I can fall into a routine. I can walk by her Majesty and barely notice her. In my most asleep moments, I don't even see her incredible eyes or hear her amazing voice. I get why couples slowly drift away from each other... We get so caught up in the demands of life, child rearing, logistics, stress, and the endless pile we are dealing with on a daily basis. Yet, if we want to feel less alone, less overwhelmed, and less stress, it is essential to find a way to make our connection, our partnership, the highest priority in our home. Only then we can meet the demands of our life more easily and fluidly. Life will not get any easier. But with a strong partnership where our lover has our back, together we can tackle just about anything, and feed off each other to gain energy and gain momentum. Don't get complacent. Wake up already. Get back in the game. Work through your challenges to find your synergy again. Don't stop. Don't even think about stopping and checking out. You can do this. I'm certain of it.

Struggling couple: "Is there a way out?"
Me: "Let me hear about your situation…"
Struggling couple: Our basic deal is this…"
They explain their really challenging situation while I listen for a while…
Me: "Ah, yes, there is a way out, of course. Your situation is very normal."
Struggling couple: "What!"
Me: "Yup. You're like most of us—we struggle in long-term relationships for a number of reasons. And we also convince ourselves that we can improve it by ourselves. So we end up struggling for years in silence because we don't want to be judged by our peers or family."
Struggling couple: "Good to know. We thought we were freaks and the only ones who have a hard time. I mean, all our friends seem happy."
Me: "Most of your friends are like you; they withhold the truth because, like you, they don't want to be seen in their weak spot and possibly face rejection or ridicule."
Struggling couple: "Right…"
Me: "So acknowledge yourselves for reaching out through your pattern of hiding, for taking a stand for yourself and for what you want. It's time to get to work, and face what is begging for your attention…"
Struggling couple: (Trembling) "Okay, let's do it…"
This couple just transitioned from a dumb couple to a smart couple.

I want to express my gratitude for those of you willing to speak openly about your challenges and how you are on the path to doing something about it. Hell *yes* to the action takers! I bow to you—to the folks who consider the option of running away (because it's so tempting), but instead choose to face that inner demon and wrestle it to the ground with love. To the people who have experienced deep pain and hurt yet get back up and learn from it, hell yes! Keep going! Please know that when you get kicked in the balls or take the metaphorical punch in the face but get back up, you give me courage and strength to tackle another layer on my own journey. You people get there's no way out but through. When you face your life like this, you're helping the rest of us feel less crazy, less alone, and we draw strength from you. So, right back at ya', warrior people! Stay in that hot fire, and master the lesson, reap the reward, turn that darkness into light, and share it with us. You got this.

There's nothing quite like sharing your life with a partner who loves you and holds you like a mountain. For us humans, that takes devotion and a tremendous effort, year in and year out. It's important to know that a deep, fulfilling, long-term relationship is available to you...yes, you. No, there is nothing "fucked up" or "wrong" with you because you don't know how to get there; you're just like me and the rest of us. You never really learned this intimacy stuff. And you have some blemishes and experiences that have caused your brain and nervous system to fire a certain way, which makes relationship extra challenging at times. That's not your fault. However, it is your responsibility to learn how to work with your internal and external challenges, and when you do, I can assure you, you can have a partner who shows up for you like a champion. So, get on it. Go after that which is possible! Stop blaming others or yourself as the reason you can't have a fulfilling partnership. Your dream relationship is in your hands. Get to work to make it a reality.

BONUS ADDITIONAL QUOTES FROM THE SMART COUPLE PODCAST TO FURTHER ILLUMINATE YOUR RELATIONSHIP JOURNEY

By the time I had finished writing this book, I had interviewed dozens and dozens of relationship "experts" on the Smart Couple Podcast. I've learned a lot from them, and they have insightful things to share with you as well. I had to include some of their wisdom in the following pages. It felt disjointed to sprinkle these quotes throughout the book, even though that was my original intention.

But rather than leave them out entirely, I felt it was essential to throw them in here as an additional bonus to you. I encourage you to go back and listen to the episode associated with the quote that speaks to you, in order to acquire a deeper transmission.

I want to sincerely thank these people for helping make the Smart Couple Podcast the greatest relationship podcast out there, especially for growth-oriented people like you.

"So often, love isn't the issue. People often say they are looking for love, but what most of us are really looking for is a partner who will go the distance with us. We want to love and be loved in a way that deepens over time and enriches our lives."

"You can hide out for years in therapy, but you can't in your relationship."

- Ellen Boeder, Psychotherapist, Faculty The Relationship School®

www.ellenboeder.com

Episode #64 **www.relationshipschool.net/podcast64**

"So here we are, wanting a relationship to succeed because we want it, but our own physiological responses, triggered by our emotional interpretations of what's going on, undermine the very relationship we're seeking. Not to mention that when those hormones are triggered and released over the long term, they make us physically and mentally ill."

"The other person cannot be and should not be your savior, except insofar as they can help you find yourself."

- Gabor Maté, Ambassador at The Relationship School®
drgabormate.com

Episode #63 **www.relationshipschool.net/podcast63**

"We are built for co-regulation of each other's nervous systems. It's more efficient than self-regulation alone."
"At the root of successful, long-term relationships is the matter of safety and security. Mature love is an outcome of partner loyalty and commitment to each other's sense of safety and security."
- Stan Tatkin,Ambassador at The Relationship School®
stantatkin.com
Episode #53 **www.relationshipschool.net/podcast53**

"Just because there is a threat, doesn't mean you need to panic, get anxious, or become fearful. You can still function, you can still cope, and deal with that challenge."
"Look for opportunities every day to feel and take in three experiences: peace, contentment, and love."
- Rick Hanson, **www.rickhanson.net**
Episode #67 **www.relationshipschool.net/podcast67**

"If you want to feel good, I cannot recommend love. If you want to feel alive—the most alive you've ever felt—then this is the game."
- Annie Lalla, **annielalla.com**
Episode #88 **www.relationshipschool.net/podcast88**

"One of the hallmarks of [fully mature sex] is the ability to be awkward and laugh at ourselves."
- David Cates, **www.facebook.com/david.cates**
Episode #16 **www.relationshipschool.net/podcast16**

"Immobilization without fear is what we call 'intimacy.' All our defenses are gone when we hold each other and are near each other. We don't need words because our bodies conform and feel safe with each other."
- Stephen Porges, **stephenporges.com**
Episode #116 **www.relationshipschool.net/podcast116**

"A lot of people aren't willing to face the loss of a bad relationship for something better. They'll hang out with the status quo and somehow talk themselves into staying, so they don't have to deal with the uncertain future."
Jeff Pincus, **www.couplestherapyboulder.com** and
Rachel Cahn, **rachelcahn.com**
Episode #112 **www.relationshipschool.net/podcast112**

"Pleasure and connection is what we want. We start to get mixed up when we place the emphasis on getting to the orgasm because we miss so much beauty that can occur within those spaces."
- Olivia Bryant, **www.oliviabryant.com.au**
Episode #96 **www.relationshipschool.net/podcast96**

"We pick partners who are close enough to our family of origin that we're thrown into the old drama. If we try to get them to change, we'll just repeat the drama. When we wake up and change our position in the old drama, that's mature love."
- Terry Real, **www.terryreal.com**
Episode #120 **www.relationshipschool.net/podcast120**

"Once we're in anxiety, our ability to connect goes offline."
- Bonnie Badenoch, **www.nurturingtheheart.com**
Episode #108 **www.relationshipschool.net/podcast108**

"When you're in 'performance' mode, you're not in connection. What women really want more than anything in the sexual experience is the feeling of connection, the feeling of intimacy and of you being 'there' with them. When you're in performance mode, you're not there with her. You're trying to figure out what to do or how to do it right. Your 'head trips' are not where great sex comes from. Learn to get out of your head and into your body."
- Destin Gerek, **destingerek.com**
Episode #98 **www.relationshipschool.net/podcast98**

"An intimate relationship is inherently disturbing."
- Bruce Tift, Episode #18
www.relationshipschool.net/podcast18

"I never understood why the hell I was making women so mad so often. I couldn't see her fear of being abandoned; all I was doing was reacting from my masculine fear of being burdened with problems I can't solve."
- Bryan Reeves, **bryanreeves.com**
Episode #94 **www.relationshipschool.net/podcast94**

"If nobody tells me how I'm showing up and how I'm impacting them, I never get the option to make a change in myself."
- Josh Levin, **www.facebook.com/joshualev**
Episode #33 **www.relationshipschool.net/podcast33**

"Everybody changes. Individuals and relationships shift. Unless you're re-upping every day, renewing that contract on a daily, weekly, monthly basis and putting the same type of effort in as when you were dating, you're on the road to divorce."
- Charles Orlando, **theproblemismen.com**
Episode #86 **www.relationshipschool.net/podcast86**

"Consciously ramping up my presence is a gift I give, not something I'm waiting for her to give."
- Satyen Raja, **satyenraja.com**
Episode #37 **www.relationshipschool.net/podcast37**

"When my partner gets curious about me in the moment, I can trust that my experience matters, my feelings matter."
- Alyson Lanier, **www.alysonlanier.com**
Episode #80 **www.relationshipschool.net/podcast80**

"When our connection is off, we stop and deal with it right now to reclaim the connection, and get back on track."
- Tripp Lanier, **www.tripplanier.com**
Episode #80 **www.relationshipschool.net/podcast80**

"The deepest spiritual work I do is in my relationship."
- John Wineland, **www.johnwineland.com**
Episode #78 **www.relationshipschool.net/podcast78**

"A couple who can take each other's perspectives, as well as perspectives from their children or perspectives from the outside, generally points to a couple who has more flexibility and more range in their relationship."
- Diane Musho Hamilton,
www.dianemushohamilton.com
Episode #20 **www.relationshipschool.net/podcast20**

"I consider it my job as a woman to both see him as presently perfect and to surrender to the future version of myself that he sees... And he does the same."
- Jennifer Russell, **www.jennifersrussell.com**
Episode #32 **www.relationshipschool.net/podcast32**

"I know that what has her upset is that she's comparing how I'm being to who she knows I can be."
- Bryan Franklin, **bryanfranklin.com**
Episode #32, **www.relationshipschool.net/podcast32**

"Early on in our relationship, it seems like we have the same values. But with money, specifically earning, saving, giving, and investing, we usually do things differently. So talk about your values and share them. How do you represent those values in the way that you spend, save, give, or invest?"
- Bari Tessler Linden, **www.baritessler.com**
Episode #90 **www.relationshipschool.net/podcast90**

"I don't believe in finding love, I don't believe in finding a partner... I believe in inspiring love, inspiring a partner."
- Adam Gilad, **www.adamgilad.com**
Episode #29 **www.relationshipschool.net/podcast29**

"The overworked entrepreneur needs a new strategy to bring to relationships. In business he's succeeded because he's doubled down on his strengths; in intimacy he will succeed more when he doubles down on his 'weaknesses' and underdeveloped parts of himself... That's where you win in love."
- Jordan Gray, **www.jordangrayconsulting.com**
Episode #130 **www.relationshipschool.net/podcast130**

"How you show up in the world determines what shows up in your world."
- Alexi Panos, **www.alexipanos.com** and Preston **Smiles, www.prestonsmiles.com**
www.bridgeexperience.com
Episode #84 **www.relationshipschool.net/podcast84**

"One of the greatest things you can do is not place your self-worth in your relationship status. If someone walks out the door, they don't take you with them. If you believe that your self-worth is at your beck and call, that you choose, it is so empowering."
- Mark Groves, **www.markgroves.tv**
Episode #128 **www.relationshipschool.net/podcast128**

"While you may fear that you might be rejected in some way, when you don't set a boundary, you lose relationship with yourself."
- Lisa Dion, **www.lisa-dion.com**
Episode #40 **www.relationshipschool.net/podcast40**

"Women expect men to act like women, and when men don't, they take it personally and explain it all from a woman's point of view."
- Alison Armstrong, **www.understandmen.com**
Episode #45 **www.relationshipschool.net/podcast45**

"If you run from a challenge, the challenge is not on the outside. The challenge is your perception of the outside, so you carry that with you. You'll just run into the challenge in another form."
- Dr. John Demartini, **www.drdemartini.com**
Episode #60 **http://www.relationshipschool.net/podcast60**

"If this is our container, then we better damn make it a crucible. And let's turn up the heat. And any sexual, relational, erotic, interpersonal desire, drive, interest, or inquiry has to have a home inside our container, or it threatens the integrity of that container."
- Jamie Wheal, **www.flowgenomeproject.com**
Episode #23 **www.relationshipschool.net/podcast23**

"Unless you schedule time to have a real conversation with your wife, you probably won't."
- Ryan Michler, **www.orderofman.com**
Episode #82 **www.relationshipschool.net/podcast82**

"The ultimate path for us is the relationship framework. My most profound experiences of divinity happened in the relational field."
- Jeff Brown, **www.soulshaping.com**
Episode #76 **www.relationshipschool.net/podcast76**

"When all of your relationships are competition-based, you never really get a chance to have true connection with somebody who can call you forward. Not call you out or push you forward, but call you forward."
- Connor Beaton, **www.mantalks.com**
Episode #73 **www.relationshipschool.net/podcast73**

"Every woman has a healthy, vibrant, wild sexuality that is delicious and passionate—no matter what her age. It can get buried, broken, lost, but it never gets destroyed."
- Layla Martin, **www.layla-martin.com/laylahome**
Episode #47 **www.relationshipschool.net/podcast47**

"Don't wait for your problems to come to you before your relationship demands your attention."
- Gaby and Raj Sundra,
www.relationshipfunandgames.com
Episode #35 **www.relationshipschool.net/podcast35**

"Sex and sexuality is a profound portal to increased self-awareness, increased authentic self-expression, and, of course, to intimacy with self, the world, and other people."
- Christiane Pelmas, **www.therewilding.com**
Episode 17 **www.relationshipschool.net/podcast17**

"Being willing to grow means being willing to encounter your own shadow as it emerges."
- Dr. Keith Witt, **www.drkeithwitt.com**
Episode #12 **www.relationshipschool.net/podcast12**

"When someone truly relaxes into who they are and gives themselves full permission to be themselves, the next natural step is to give other people permission to be who they are."
- Joel Mark Witt and Antonia Dodge,
www.personalityhacker.com
Episode #77 **www.relationshipschool.net/podcast77**

ACKNOWLEDGMENTS

Thank you, Mom and Dad, for raising me exactly as you did and awakening in me the desire to learn about relationships. I am forever grateful for your love, mishaps, care, and everything in between. I love you both deeply. Please know you parented me just right.

Thank you to the following folks who helped me put this little book together. Each of these people helped me in little and big ways:

Macon McIntyre for helping collect these quotes off my Facebook wall, Tripp Lanier for modeling how to create a good podcast, Charles Busker for some basic podcast tech questions, Max Nachamkin for the first guy to show me how to use Screenflow with my Mac (which helps me record the podcast) Melina Seeto for scanning Facebook, organizing, formatting, editing, and loving me through this process. Steve Stroitir for having a keen visual sense of style on the Smart Couple logo, fonts, and graphics as well as co-designing the book cover, Rachel Van Lant for little helpful writing nudges here and there, Nicholas Traugott for pulling the guest quotes together and designing quote boxes for Instagram and social media, Jeffrey Platts for helping with the podcast and extracting some of the guest quotes, Dan Cugliari for being our main podcast beast and having a sense of what I want with each guest quote and all our show notes, Julianna Barbieri for helping operate the business and helping me get organized so a project like this can happen, Alyssa Morin for helping my business get off the ground...

And of course, thank you to my wife Ellen:

You are my main teacher and you take me to school year after year. No one has taught me more about an intimate relationship than you. It is a true honor to be your husband, your sounding board, and a witness to the deep transformation you have undergone since being initiated into marriage and motherhood. Being a co-parent with you, Ellen, is the greatest accomplishment of my life by far. I'm inspired by your courage to meet life with such audacious and intelligent questions. Such deep surrender. I love how you allow yourself to be sculpted by your experience, over and over. I cannot thank you enough for being my sounding board, my mountain, my rock, my best friend, my secure home base, and my wife. Your challenge and support has carried me through the darkness and confusion every time. I'm a stronger adult man thanks to you. And, wow, none of this would be possible without you fighting for and believing in our deep, radical love. Thank you for diving so deep for you, me, and for our beautiful children. I'm grateful I burned my fear to the ground, so I could marry you. And I'm grateful you chose me over and over and called me forward. Thank you for believing in us and seeing what I couldn't see, right from the start. Without you leading the way here, this book and the concepts therein, along with The Relationship School®, wouldn't be a reality. Damn. Thank you doesn't begin to describe how I feel here. I love how we roll and I love how you continue to help me embrace more of who I am. Thank you, dear. I love you.

ABOUT THE AUTHOR

Jayson Gaddis, relationship student and teacher, host of the Smart Couple Podcast, and founder of The Relationship School® is on a mission to teach people the one class they didn't get in school: "How to create a safe, sexy, and successful romantic relationship." He was emotionally constipated for years before relationship failure forced him to turn his life over to learning about relationships. Now, after two painful breakups and trying to run away, he's married to his amazing wife of 10 years and has two beautiful kids. When he doesn't live and breathe this stuff with his family, he pretty much gets his ass handed to him.

Jayson has developed several successful online products including End Your Struggle With Him, Conflict Relief, Indestructible Partnerships, Relationship as a Path, and now the infamous Deep Psychology of Intimate Relationships, the two-semester course on relationships you should have received in high school or college. Jayson also runs one of the deepest, most comprehensive relationship coaches training programs on the planet.

Jayson started The Relationship School®[1] because he got tired of complaining that there was no such class in our current school system. Now, there's a place for you to formally learn and practice the skills required to have a safe, fulfilling partnership over time.

He currently lives in Boulder Colorado with his wife Ellen and their two cosmic kids.

A POWERFUL ADDITIONAL RESOURCE

Want to meet other readers, podcast listeners, and growth-oriented people like you?

Join our free Facebook group to meet others, share challenges and victories, and learn.

Ask to join this private group. Once accepted, introduce yourself and share your favorite quote along with the page number. See you in there!

www.jaysongaddis.com/smartcouplegroup

EVALUATE THE CURRENT HEALTH OF YOUR RELATIONSHIP

Download the Relationship Scorecard™ here:

www.relationshipschool.net/scorecard

---

[1] http://www.relationshipschool.net/

WHERE TO FIND JAYSON GADDIS

www.jaysongaddis.com

www.relationshipschool.net

www.facebook.com/jaysongaddisfanpage

www.instagram.com/jaysongaddis

www.twitter.com/jaygaddis

www.youtube.com/user/Jaysongaddis

WANT TO SHARE THE LOVE?

Visit our Store for apparel. 2% of all sales go toward helping teens and young adults learn how to create safe, sexy, successful Romantic Relationships:

www.relationshipschool.net/store

GET BOOK DISCOUNTS AND DEALS

Get discounts and special deals on our bestselling books at
www.tckpublishing.com/bookdeals